Mapping with ArcGIS Pro

Design accurate and user-friendly maps to share the story of your data

Amy Rock
Ryan Malhoski

BIRMINGHAM - MUMBAI

Mapping with ArcGIS Pro

Commissioning Editor: Merint Mathew
Acquisition Editor: Karan Sadawana
Content Development Editor: Priyanka Sawant
Technical Editor: Gaurav Gala
Copy Editor: Safis Editing
Project Coordinator: Vaidehi Sawant
Proofreader: Safis Editing
Indexer: Rekha Nair
Graphics: Jason Monteiro
Production Coordinator: Shantanu Zagade

First published: March 2018

Production reference: 1070318

Published by Packt Publishing Ltd.
Livery Place
35 Livery Street
Birmingham
B3 2PB, UK.

ISBN 978-1-78829-800-1

www.packtpub.com

Special thanks to the many students over the years who have pushed beyond GIS defaults and into the world of carto-niftiness. Your eagerness to learn and desire to succeed have led you to many places around the world, where you have helped spread the demand for effective and appealing GIS maps. And to HHLB and my colleagues at NACIS, thank you for sharing the joy of kartenvergnügen.

– Amy Rock

Special thanks to the many people at Esri that have worked hard to release a modern software package to allow people to disseminate geographic data to the masses via paper and the web. Also, a thank you to the educators that pushed me to spread the value of GIS and work for the greater good.

– Ryan Malhoski

`mapt.io`

Mapt is an online digital library that gives you full access to over 5,000 books and videos, as well as industry leading tools to help you plan your personal development and advance your career. For more information, please visit our website.

Why subscribe?

- Spend less time learning and more time coding with practical eBooks and Videos from over 4,000 industry professionals

- Improve your learning with Skill Plans built especially for you

- Get a free eBook or video every month

- Mapt is fully searchable

- Copy and paste, print, and bookmark content

PacktPub.com

Did you know that Packt offers eBook versions of every book published, with PDF and ePub files available? You can upgrade to the eBook version at `www.PacktPub.com` and as a print book customer, you are entitled to a discount on the eBook copy. Get in touch with us at `service@packtpub.com` for more details.

At `www.PacktPub.com`, you can also read a collection of free technical articles, sign up for a range of free newsletters, and receive exclusive discounts and offers on Packt books and eBooks.

Contributors

About the authors

Dr. Amy Rock is a community geographer and an avid proponent of community leadership. Her research and projects include using GIS to examine economic relationships, economic accessibility, public participation in the federal block grant process, and commercial government GIS projects. She is currently teaching on the award-winning cartography program at Humboldt State University, and she is a director of their Online Geospatial Certificate Program.

Many thanks to Craig Williams, of Esri, for his ongoing efforts to continually improve ArcGIS Pro (and respond to my feedback), and to Kenneth Field and John Nelson, also of Esri, for their carto-evangelism on making beautiful maps with GIS software. Thanks also to the late Dr. Hubertus Bloemer, who instilled cartographic principles in me, and reminded me never to relax my standards for the sake of faster maps.

Ryan Malhoski is a GIS developer with over 10 years of GIS experience. He has a bachelor's degree in GIS and urban planning from Sacramento State University. He is currently a GIS developer for the City of Sacramento in the enterprise applications division. He spent over 6 years working for the U.S. Army Corps of Engineers as a geographer, where he was the GIS lead and project manager for multiple civil works and military projects. Ryan volunteers for Code for Sacramento, a brigade of Code for America, where he has volunteered for 2 years and just recently became Captain of the brigade.

I would to thank those who were supportive of me through the process of writing this book. Thank you to my amazing fiancee, Maggie, my personal cheerleader, for her support and guidance through the writing process. Without her, I could've never met this challenge. Thank you to my extremely supportive family, Walter, Patti, and Sonja, who helped foster my love for technology. Thank you to my coworker, Dara O'Beirne, for introducing me to this opportunity and convincing me that I could accomplish this. Finally, I would like to thank my dog "Big Man" Baxter for keeping my feet warm while writing late into the night and forcing me to have play breaks.

About the reviewer

Dara O'Beirne is a certified GIS Professional with over 12 years of GIS and Python experience. He has coauthored *ArcPy and ArcGIS, Second Edition*, published by Packt. He earned both his bachelor's and master's of art in geography from the San Francisco State University. Currently a GIS analyst working at the City of Sacramento's Department of Utilities. He was also an integral part of the GIS Team working on developing a web mapping application used during each event at the new Levi's Stadium.

> *I would like to thank my wife, Kate, and my daughters, Anya and Brynn, and tell them that I love them. I would like to thank my family, who has always guided and supported me, from Ireland to America and beyond. I would like to thank my professors at San Francisco State University, and all of my colleagues and friends who have helped me along the way.*

Packt is searching for authors like you

If you're interested in becoming an author for Packt, please visit `authors.packtpub.com` and apply today. We have worked with thousands of developers and tech professionals, just like you, to help them share their insight with the global tech community. You can make a general application, apply for a specific hot topic that we are recruiting an author for, or submit your own idea.

Table of Contents

Preface

Making maps in GIS software has always been challenging, and books about making maps with GIS focus on tools rather than design principles. ArcGIS Pro makes it easier than ever to make attractive maps without resorting to an external graphics program, but without good designs, it's still possible to make bad maps. This book integrates the basics of cartographic design with hands-on activities to help develop your skills with the interface and functionality of ArcGIS Pro.

Who this book is for

This book is intended for GIS professionals who are new to ArcGIS Pro and want to improve the quality of the maps they make. This book will also be useful for those who are transitioning from ArcMap to ArcGIS Pro and are trying to translate all the things they are used to doing into the new platform. Basic familiarity with geospatial data and file management, as well as an understanding of how GIS layers work, will be helpful.

What this book covers

Chapter 1, *How Maps Get Made*, lays the foundation of how a great map is made. You will learn how to take into account the audience of the map, how to search for and review data from authoritative sources, and how to create a quick and simple map with just a few clicks using ArcGIS Pro.

Chapter 2, *Getting Started in ArcGIS Pro*, covers navigating the new interface, adding and organizing data layers, and understanding the new Map and Layout views. We'll make a basic map and learn how to use the Symbology pane, duplicate layers for cartographic effect, and create bookmarks for consistent extent. In the Layout view, we'll work with multiple map frames, add map elements, and set page configurations for sharing our map via print or digital media.

Chapter 3, *Organizing the Page Structure*, is all about balance. We'll discuss the key principles of map design, how to tailor the map layout to improve visual communication, and help our map reader focus on what we need them to see. We'll take a deeper look at using multiple data frames to add clarity and scope or create small multiples, and you'll learn how to plan it all out to create an effective, impactful map layout.

Chapter 4, *Typographic Principles*, looks at one of the most heavily-used but frequently neglected aspects of a map: labels. We'll start with a basic overview of letterforms and fonts, with an eye to developing mood, and building on the hierarchy we developed in the previous chapter. The development of map grammar is as important as ensuring legibility, and understanding font relationships is key. We'll also apply classic label positioning principles for improved readability, and we'll customize ArcPro's dynamic labeling to do the heavy lifting.

Chapter 5, *Picking Colors with Confidence*, moves beyond default color palettes and into the world of custom colors and using color with purpose. We'll dive into how color works in both print and digital forms and learn how to set color modes and custom colors in ArcGIS Pro. We'll explore the meaning of warm and cool colors and how to use them together for maximum impact. We'll also take a quick look at the principles of color theory and color as a visual variable, before building and importing color schemes. We will then take advantage of Pro's improved rendering to work with transparencies in sophisticated ways. Last but not least, you'll learn how color and mood are related, and look at design for color acuity to ensure effective communication with our map's reader.

Chapter 6, *All Maps Are Approximations of Reality*, discusses how it is rare to find perfect data. You will learn how you can make small changes to data to make it more legible, have more meaning for your audience, and reduce confusion. You'll learn about different popular styles of maps and how to properly choose a style to fit your needs. You will learn how to avoid a common pitfall of data: aggregating data without normalizing it. Lastly, you'll learn how to create and use hex bins to aggregate geographic data, and how it is a better aggregation method than others.

Chapter 7, *Understanding and Choosing Projections*, primes you on how coordinate systems and projections can have drastic effects on the shape and accuracy of your data. You'll learn that even though there is no one single perfect projection, you can easily choose the right projection for your data and map once you understand the basic concepts of geodesy. You'll learn how to use the easy-to-use tools in ArcGIS Pro to help you select appropriate projections and quickly switch between them to compare the outputs. Lastly, you'll learn about Z or elevation, how important it is, and how it can cause real-world problems when not handled correctly.

Chapter 8, *Clean Symbology and Uncluttered Maps*, covers using and creating symbols that are intuitive and easy to read. We'll look at scales of measurement related to symbology, and visual variables for points, lines, and polygons. A quick dive into classifying data with choropleths, graduated and proportional symbols, in which we discuss both, the potential and pitfalls of these methods of data visualization. We'll wrap up with Pro's attribute-driven symbology and controlling visibility at scale, two great tools for making your map design dynamic with less effort.

Chapter 9, *Getting Started with ArcGIS Online*, demonstrates the ins and outs of the powerful web GIS platform that Esri provides. You'll learn how organizations, groups, and users are managed, how data is managed and utilized, and how to use ArcGIS Pro to connect and interact with ArcGIS Online. You will learn how to interact with the 2D web maps and 3D scenes that you can use to visualize and present your data. Lastly, you'll learn how to publish data from ArcGIS Pro to ArcGIS Online to share with the world.

Chapter 10, *Leveraging Esri Smart Mapping*, builds upon what you learned in the preceding chapter and how you can let ArcGIS Online's smart mapping help you make decisions on how to visualize your data properly. You'll learn about the different methods of analyzing and visualizing data that help you tell your story. Lastly, you'll learn about the new powerful expression language, Arcade, which allows you to create dynamic data using simple expressions that you can symbolize of.

To get the most out of this book

You'll need the following:

- An ArcGIS Pro license
- An ArcGIS Online account
- Internet access

Download the example code files

You can download the example code files for this book from your account at www.packtpub.com. If you purchased this book elsewhere, you can visit www.packtpub.com/support and register to have the files emailed directly to you.

You can download the code files by following these steps:

1. Log in or register at `www.packtpub.com`.
2. Select the **SUPPORT** tab.
3. Click on **Code Downloads & Errata**.
4. Enter the name of the book in the **Search** box and follow the onscreen instructions.

Once the file is downloaded, please make sure that you unzip or extract the folder using the latest version of:

- WinRAR/7-Zip for Windows
- Zipeg/iZip/UnRarX for Mac
- 7-Zip/PeaZip for Linux

The code bundle for the book is also hosted on GitHub at `https://github.com/PacktPublishing/Mapping-with-ArcGIS-Pro`. In case there's an update to the code, it will be updated on the existing GitHub repository.

We also have other code bundles from our rich catalog of books and videos available at `https://github.com/PacktPublishing/`. Check them out!

Download the color images

We also provide a PDF file that has color images of the screenshots/diagrams used in this book. You can download it here: `https://www.packtpub.com/sites/default/files/downloads/MappingwithArcGISPRo_ColorImages.pdf`.

Conventions used

There are a number of text conventions used throughout this book.

`CodeInText`: Indicates code words in text, database table names, folder names, filenames, file extensions, pathnames, dummy URLs, user input, and Twitter handles. Here is an example: "Once signed in, you are asked to create a new project. You'll want to choose the `Map.aptx` template."

A block of code is set as follows:

```
Your name
Today's date
Source: Esri
```

Bold: Indicates a new term, an important word, or words that you see onscreen. For example, words in menus or dialog boxes appear in the text like this. Here is an example: "To create a layout, click **Insert** from the top of the **ArcGIS Pro** ribbon, click **New Layout**, then choose **Letter** under **ANSI Landscape**."

Warnings or important notes appear like this.

Tips and tricks appear like this.

Get in touch

Feedback from our readers is always welcome.

General feedback: Email `feedback@packtpub.com` and mention the book title in the subject of your message. If you have questions about any aspect of this book, please email us at `questions@packtpub.com`.

Errata: Although we have taken every care to ensure the accuracy of our content, mistakes do happen. If you have found a mistake in this book, we would be grateful if you would report this to us. Please visit `www.packtpub.com/submit-errata`, selecting your book, clicking on the Errata Submission Form link, and entering the details.

Piracy: If you come across any illegal copies of our works in any form on the Internet, we would be grateful if you would provide us with the location address or website name. Please contact us at `copyright@packtpub.com` with a link to the material.

If you are interested in becoming an author: If there is a topic that you have expertise in and you are interested in either writing or contributing to a book, please visit `authors.packtpub.com`.

Reviews

Please leave a review. Once you have read and used this book, why not leave a review on the site that you purchased it from? Potential readers can then see and use your unbiased opinion to make purchase decisions, we at Packt can understand what you think about our products, and our authors can see your feedback on their book. Thank you!

For more information about Packt, please visit packtpub.com.

1
How Maps Get Made

It was only a short time ago that the visualization of **geographic information system** (**GIS**) data was almost exclusively physical, data was hard to come by, and the audience of a map was a single person or a small group or community. The pervasiveness of web mapping in recent years shows that the general public is getting more accustomed to static and dynamic maps showing more than the route from A to B. In this chapter, you will learn how to tailor your map to your audience, find authoritative data to support what you are trying to convey, and create a work plan to structure your data in an organized way to create the best mapping product.

In this chapter, we will cover the following topics:

- Knowing your audience
- Setting yourself up for a great map
- The importance of data management
- Finding authoritative datasets
- Outlining the work ahead

Knowing your audience

While every mapmaker strives to make the most visually appealing map they can imagine, you have to remember that the purpose of a map is to convey data clearly to your audience. In my career, I have made maps for planners, engineers, rangers, hydrologists, lawyers, field crews, surveyors, elected officials, and the public, just to name a few. If I was working on one project that involved all of those groups, each map of that project would be different than the other. Finding out *who the audience of a map is?* should be one of your first objectives.

With this figured out, you have a clearer goal of what data you will need and how to show it. Don't be afraid to ask questions; a lot of times you can be pulled into a project in which you have no background. It is more appropriate to ask a lot of questions in the beginning, rather than in the middle or towards the end of a project.

I typically ask the following questions when I get pulled into a project:

- Who is the audience of the map?
- What are you trying to show?
- Does any data already exist?
- Will there be any analysis?
- Will this be updated regularly to show progress/change?

With these questions answered, I can usually feel comfortable enough to start a project. This will help me form a guide on how to formulate a work plan to solve this mapping problem.

Clear expectations

Because mapping is becoming more accessible to people, there is a higher demand for it. People understand the power of showing data on a map, but may not understand the complexity of creating a great map. It is important to lay out realistic expectations when creating a map. It is really easy to put too much information into a map, which will only confuse the audience, and make the map look poor, as well. Not that it's impossible to have a lot of data in your map; it just takes a lot longer than most people expect and skills learned over many years of cartography experience.

A lot of people, myself included, can get excited about a project and want to immediately start working on it. Going out looking for any and all data or starting the design of the layout may be exciting, but this eagerness can cost you in the long run, as you will perform work that might not be used in the project. The beginning of a mapping project should move slowly at first, to mitigate unnecessary work.

Setting yourself up for a great map

ArcGIS Pro is a powerful desktop software that has been built from the ground up to allow a GIS professional to have a single place to deliver mapping products across multiple platforms. ArcGIS Pro was designed to be easier to approach for those who may have not come up using the soon to be legacy ArcGIS for Desktop suite. ArcGIS Pro uses a more scalable project management model from the beginning. This new model sets you up with an environment to store, reference, or process project-relevant data logically in multiple workspaces under one project.

For instance, with ArcGIS Desktop, you would have one map layout per MXD file. In a project that may need multiple maps, you would have to create an MXD for each map. Typically, you would store relevant MXDs with each other in a folder system on your local machine, or more preferably, a network drive. You would have to run multiple instances of ArcMap to make changes to them all, and unless you explicitly saved it, all the data connections and toolbars would stay on your local machine. With ArcGIS Pro, you store all your maps, workspaces, and data connections in one project in the .aprx file. That makes it easier for you or someone else to open the project up somewhere else and have the same environment.

Data management is important

Before you start working on your project, you need to set up a logical folder and file-naming convention. This is a very important step, because as you may have experienced in the past, you can get pulled into something else and shelve a project for a length of time and lose a lot of memory of how things were done. This also helps in case someone else has to come in and pick up where you left off.

Project folder structure

If your organization has a defined folder structure on how to manage folders and files, use that structure, but if you are given a free range, I highly recommend coming up with a folder structure that will help you keep files organized. In the past, most of everything was in the shapefile format, so you would typically organize by the theme of the data. Today, ArcGIS Pro will automatically create a geodatabase file when you create a new project, giving you a place to store your project data. I will usually create another geodatabase file to be my scratch area and leave the original geodatabase file as my final project data.

Whenever I receive data from someplace, I start a folder called `original` and create a folder with the name of the source and make the files read-only. This has saved me a few times when I received or found data, made a change to it and couldn't revert. Now I don't have to remember where I got the data or find the person who sent it to me originally. I usually create folders for each type of file I receive, for example, `KML`, `LYRX`, `SHP`, `raster`, and so on.

If you feel comfortable with a folder structure already, by all means, use it; just keep it consistent! Consistency is key when organizing things.

Project file naming

Just like making sure your folder structure is organized in a logical way, your file naming must follow a logical pattern to be successful. We've all been there, running geoprocesses all day, sometimes tweaking settings multiple times. At the end, you see all the files with the suffixes `_export`, `_export2`, `_clip`, `_merge`, and so on, and if you have a program crash or a forced restart, you will have a hard time trying to figure out which one you were using. Forcing yourself to take the five seconds to change the filename to something more descriptive will save many seconds/minutes/hours down the line. What I show will be a guide; change it as you need to, and just remember to be consistent!

My four keys to file naming:

- No spaces or special characters
- Use camel case or snake case
- When including a date, use a date prefix like `yyyymmdd`
- If processing data, enter the process name and any major settings (for example, `20171002_City_Limits_Buffer_10mi`)

While today's software is smart enough to ignore spaces or special characters, there is still legacy software that will fail because of them. An added benefit of not using spaces is when you send a network path of a file or folder to someone, a link will automatically be generated in most email clients. If there is a space in the URL, it may create a link using all the characters up to the space, creating an invalid link. Use camel or snake case for legibility, and when appropriate, use the `yyyymmdd` date prefix. Having the date in that format allows you to sort by name and have the dated data show chronologically. Finally, putting in the process name with major settings allows you to quickly and easily find the particular data you processed. Now that we have thought about our folder structure and file-naming conventions, let's put them to use by finding data to populate our project!

Finding authoritative datasets

Sharing GIS data was a difficult proposition in the past, as if you didn't have your own infrastructure, there wasn't a central place where people could share GIS data. This meant that most data lived as a hyperlink to a .zip file of a shapefile or a .kmz file, being hidden deep within a website not devoted to GIS. The age of the file was sometimes unknown, because there was no metadata or nothing on the website that told you whether the files were being updated or when they were created. With the introduction of ArcGIS Online, people and organizations have a central place where they can share GIS data and give the burden of hosting and serving the data to **Esri**. There are also many websites that use open-source solutions to serve out data in the form of a **web mapping service** (**WMS**) or a **web feature service** (**WFS**).

 Just like everything on the internet, don't automatically assume data is correct. There's a lot of bad data out there. Unsure about a dataset? Try contacting the person or organization who created it.

Searching the web for authoritative data

With GIS being more accessible, and with more demand for GIS data, it truly is a good time for the GIS professional. However, you must be wary of datasets—How they were created? If they are maintained? And/or whether the data is complete or not? Inspect every dataset to find:

- Metadata, if available
- Who created the data?
- Do field names make sense, or do you need a key/lookup table for them?
- What scale was the data drawn at?
- What is the accuracy, spatially and mathematically?
- What is the licensing of the data?

These are some of the questions you should ask yourself when searching out data online.

Not all of your data needs are going to be useful as static files on your file server or local machine. It may be that the data you need is too large or changes so often you'd rather not have to go out every day/week/month to download the newest version. There is a lot of dynamic data being served out in the web, so when you access it, you are always getting the most up-to-date data and only getting the data you need. Not having to store the data locally and being able to just pull the data from a server can be very advantageous. For example, if you want to create a map showing the current weather, it may not be necessary to keep the weather data for a historical archive. The purpose of the map is to show current weather, so you pull live data from a governmental body or commercial provider to overlay your map. That way, if it's a web map, you don't have to worry about keeping things up to date, and if it's a layer in a static map, every time you export or print it will show the updated data. This works well when GIS is needed in an operations center where a large map is printed every so often.

Some of the biggest GIS data creators are governments. Many governments produce a whole lot of data, but most have one flaw. They don't advertise it well. Thankfully, search engine crawlers do a great job of digging deep into complex government websites and allowing us to search for the keywords we are looking for. Adding keywords like shapefile, geodatabase, GIS, REST, WMS, and WFS to what you are trying to find can make searching quicker. In the United States, you can use `https://data.gov` to search against a large amount of federal, state, county, and local data. In Europe, you have `https://data.europa.eu` or `https://www.europeandataportal.eu`.

ArcGIS Online

Esri has a data repository called the **Living Atlas**, which contains curated data from Esri that you can use in your maps. The majority of these datasets are available to the public, but there are a few datasets in **Living Atlas** that are either subscriber content or premium content. The last two types of **Living Atlas** datasets require you to have an ArcGIS organizational account and/or credits available. Warning! Be careful with credit consumption; it can add up real quick and can drain your organization's credits. You can access the **Living Atlas** data two ways:

- Through ArcGIS Pro
- At `https://arcgis.com`

In ArcGIS Pro, you can access the data through the **Catalog** pane under **Portal** by clicking on the icon with the book on top of a cloud, shown as the following:

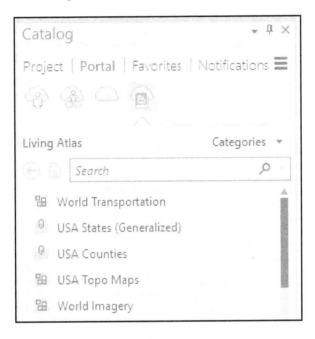

Figure 1.1: Living Atlas Data in ArcGIS Pro

You can also search for **Living Atlas** on ArcGIS Online to find datasets. A great feature of ArcGIS Online is being able to find a layer there and open it within ArcGIS Pro automatically. We will go into more depth on this in `Chapter 9`, *Get Started with ArcGIS Online*. ArcGIS Online also has data from people and organizations around the world. Because they chose to leverage ArcGIS Online to host their data, you can be sure that it will come into your map in ArcGIS Pro with little to no configuration. ArcGIS Pro was designed around consuming data from GIS servers just as much as it was designed for local data.

Outlining the work ahead

Since beginning this chapter, you have already asked a lot of questions, and have hopefully received all your answers so that you can begin working on your map or maps. You have considered who the audience of the map is, what you need to show, that data already exists, and if you will need to recreate this map later.

You will finish off the rest of this chapter going through a scenario where you need to create a map for a report that your marketing manager is putting together. The marketing manager needs a simple map showing the population density of all the states of the contiguous United States (lower 48) and Alaska, using a single color ramp to fit on a US letter-size paper in landscape. The marketing manager said that it just needs to be a basic map, as the focus will be on the report and not the map. This is a quick and easy task in ArcGIS Pro.

First, let's open **ArcGIS Pro** and sign in:

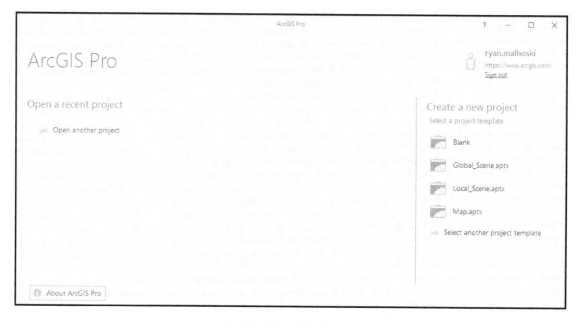

Figure 1.2: ArcGIS Pro initial screen

After signing in, we need to follow the following steps:

1. Once signed in, you are asked to create a new project. You'll want to choose the `Map.aptx` template.

2. Let's make sure to give a descriptive name for this map. You want to be able to tell what it is for just by looking at the filename. Let's call this `PopulationDensityForMarketingReport` and store it in a folder for our ArcGIS projects.

3. Leave the checkbox checked to create a new folder for this `Map` project.

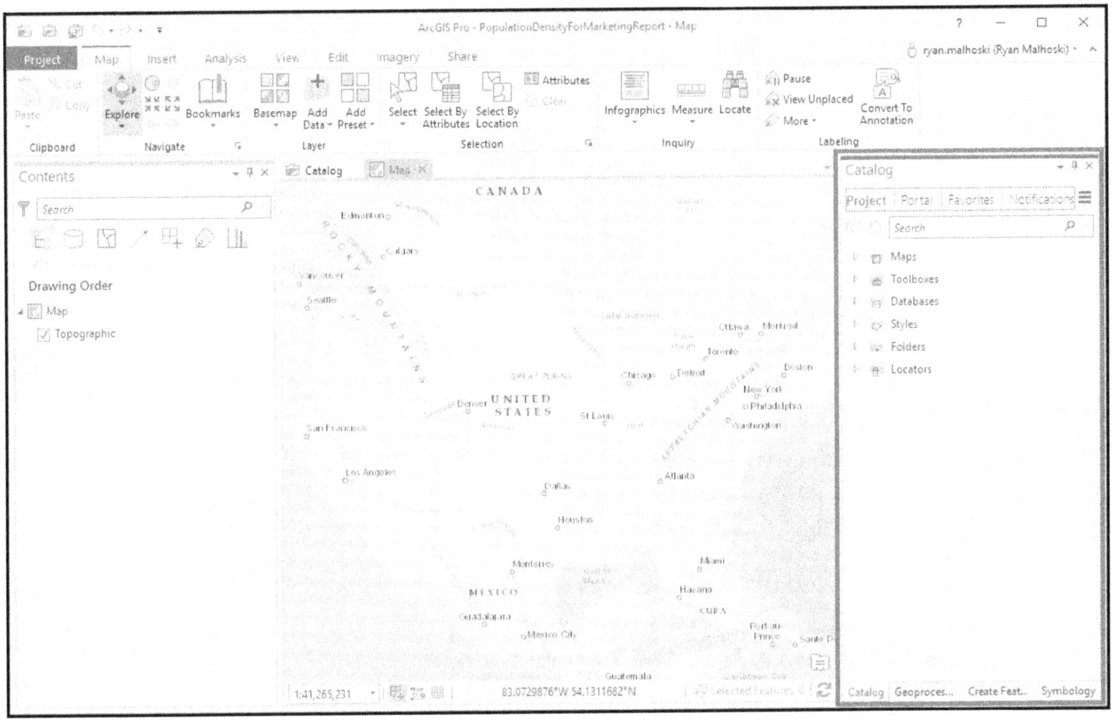

Figure 1.3: Initial map in the Map.aprx template with the Catalog pane highlighted in red

You now have a simple map showing the United States. Now you need to find your state data, with population density. Luckily, ArcGIS Online's **Living Atlas** that you learned about earlier has the data you need:

1. To find it, go to the **Catalog** pane on the right and click **Portal**.
2. Click on the icon with the green book on top of a cloud (shown in *Figure 1.1*).
3. Once the **Living Atlas** data is populated, you will see an item called **USA States (Generalized)**; right-click it and select **Add to Current Map**.

4. This will bring the data into the map's table of contents. You will need to expand the **USA States (Generalized)** layer and right-click the **USA_States_Generalized** item and select **Attribute Table** to open up the attribute table. You will see the table pop up from the bottom, and you can inspect the fields available:

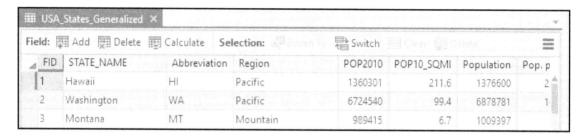

FID	STATE_NAME	Abbreviation	Region	POP2010	POP10_SQMI	Population	Pop. p
1	Hawaii	HI	Pacific	1360301	211.6	1376600	2
2	Washington	WA	Pacific	6724540	99.4	6878781	1
3	Montana	MT	Mountain	989415	6.7	1009397	

Figure 1.4: Attribute table

After looking at the fields, we can see a field called **POP10_SQMI,** which gives you the population per square mile from 2010. This was the data your market manager was looking for. Now you just need to symbolize the states using a single color ramp:

1. To do this, you right-click **USA_States_Generalized,** and then click **Symbology.**
2. The pane on the right side of **ArcGIS Pro** will show you the symbology properties of the **USA_States_Generalized** layer, as seen in the following screenshot:

Figure 1.5: Symbology properties

3. Click in the drop-down where it says **Single Symbol** and change it to **Graduated Colors**. You will see the map change and see that you now have new settings in the **Symbology Properties** pane.

4. Since you want to show the population density, you should change the drop-down next to **Field** to **POP10_SQMI**. Choose a single color ramp of your choice, and you are almost ready to send out this map.

You have put data into a map, but right now, the map isn't put into a layout. A layout is where you would insert your map and other items, like a legend, scale bar, north arrow, and title:

1. To create a layout, click **Insert** from the top of the **ArcGIS Pro** ribbon, click **New Layout**, then choose **Letter** under **ANSI Landscape**. A new window will appear with the title **Layout**. Right now it is blank, because we have yet to insert your map into it.

2. To insert your map, you will click the icon above **Map Frame**. You now see the map with your data, and luckily, it shows the data to an extent where you can see the contiguous United States and Alaska. Now you just need to insert a north arrow, scale bar, and title.

3. To insert a north arrow, click the **North Arrow** icon; this will place a basic north arrow into your layout. Let's move it to the bottom-left corner of the map; to do this, click and hold on the north arrow, then drag it to the lower-left corner.

4. You will need to add a scale bar by clicking the **Scale Bar** icon, next to where the **North Arrow** icon was. This will add a scale bar to the middle of the map; you will move it to the bottom-left corner of the map, just like you did with the north arrow.

5. You will need to add a legend so the reader knows what the colors mean. To insert a legend, click the **Legend** icon. Unlike the north arrow and scale bar, you will click and drag within the layout to insert your legend. You will place the legend in the top-right corner of the map, where you have a bit of room. Click the top-right corner of the map and drag down to the left to create the legend. You can resize it if it's too small or too large.

6. You need to change the layer label and field label to look a little nicer in the legend and be more descriptive. To do this, expand the **Map Frame** item in the contents pane. Perform a slow double-click on **USA_States_Generalized** and change it to **States**. Then perform a slow double-click on **POP10_SQMI** and change it to **Population per square mile**.

7. Finally, you need a title. To create one, click the **Text** icon in the **Insert** ribbon, which is a white square with the symbol **Aa**. In the drop-down menu, select **Title Large (Sans Serif)**. Then click **Text** next to the white square and click right above the map in the white space and start typing **2010 Population Density by State**, then click the white space of the map. Click and drag the text so that it is centered over the map.

8. Now you need to export the map to PDF. To do this, click **Share** in the ribbon, then click **Layout**, which has a green arrow icon. Navigate to your project directory and name the file
`PopulationDensityMapLandscapeAnsiLetter.pdf`.

By following these steps, you have created the map that the marketing manager was looking for. While this map may not win any cartographic contests, it clearly shows the data requested, and we have a descriptive title. Not every map needs to be a perfect cartographic product. The best map is one that clearly shows the author's message:

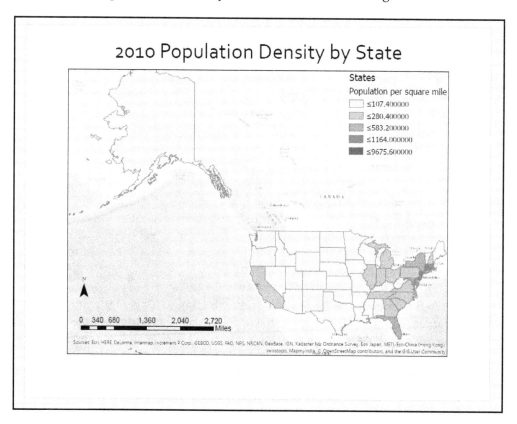

Figure 1.6: Our final map

Summary

In this chapter, you learned to make sure you know your audience, what questions to ask, and what expectations to set when starting a mapping project. You learned the value of proper folder structure and naming conventions. You learned how to source authoritative data from a few places, and finally, you put all that knowledge into making a quick map for your marketing manager.

In the next chapter, you will go more in-depth on how to use ArcGIS Pro and how to make better looking maps with more advanced settings.

2
Getting Started in ArcGIS Pro

An important part of any map creation is good data organization. This begins with good file management and continues with managing layers in your workspace. As we noted in `Chapter 1`, *How Maps Get Made*, good file naming and organizational practices are critical to streamlining your mapping process. If you are working on your computer's hard drive, you may wish to set up a folder dedicated to your ArcPro projects (for example, `C:\ArcProProjects`). If you are working in an organizational server environment, create a folder according to your organization's file management policies.

ArcPro allows you to organize your project through the **Contents** pane, the **Map View**, and the **Layout View**. The **Contents** pane allows you to list your data layers in a variety of ways by drawing order, data source, and more. The **Map View**, like the **Data View** in ArcMap, is where you can see your data layers from a single **Map Frame,** geographically aligned and as they will appear in your final map. The **Layout View** is where you will assemble your final map output (with one or more map frames), add map elements, and finalize output for print or screen. In this chapter, we'll look at each in detail and practice organizing data for cartographic purposes.

A key feature of ArcPro is the ability to easily interface with ArcGIS Online and share data within your organization or publicly. Its new project file format also allows you to create multiple layouts with the same map frame and reuse map frames and layouts in multiple projects, which can save you time if you work with the same data regularly.

In this chapter, we will be covering the following topics:

- Opening a project
- Organizing the Contents pane
- Working in the Map View
- Transitioning to the Layout View
- Creating a map output

Opening a project

Let's open an existing project and take a look at the ArcPro interface. When you first launch the application, you'll be asked to sign in with your ArcGIS Online account (if you don't want to sign in each time, check **Sign me in automatically**).

 If you will be working without an internet connection, you can check out a license for up to 30 days from the licensing settings.

On the opening screen, select **Open another project**. From the folder where you installed the sample data, select **GettingStarted**:

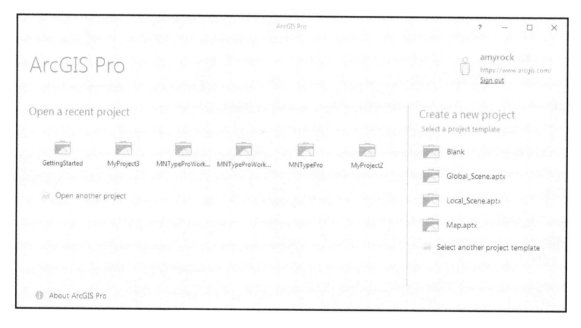

Figure 2.1: The ArcGIS Pro startup window

Once your project opens, it may look familiar to you if you use Microsoft Office. This is not accidental, but part of a collaboration between Esri and Microsoft. Across the top, you'll find the ribbon and tabs (**Project**, **Map**, **Insert**, **Analysis**, **View**, **Edit**, **Imagery**, and **Share**) in one or more panes. The panes and ribbon are context-sensitive and will change depending on what tools or features are selected. The bottom half of the window is still fairly similar to ArcMap. At the left is the **Contents** pane.

To the right is the **Map View.** (If you do not see the **Contents** pane, it may be turned off. To turn it on, click **View | Contents**). If you are familiar with ArcMap's interface and functionality, you may find the

page `http://pro.arcgis.com/en/pro-app/get-started/migrate-to-arcgis-pro.htm` helpful:

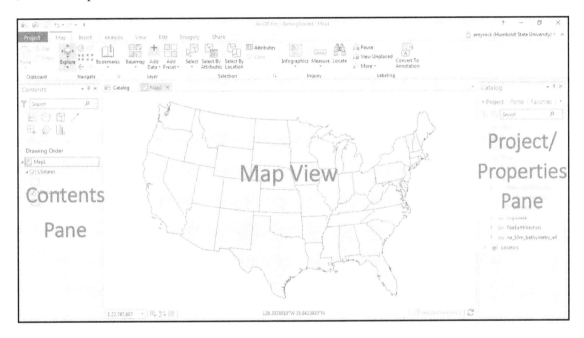

Figure 2.2: The ArcPro work environment

Organizing the Contents pane

Within the **Contents** pane, the information is organized into a nested or tree structure. The top-level is the name of this particular map. Underneath it are the various layers or files that make up this map, listed in a particular order, determined by the selection chosen under the search box. Since we're viewing our layers by drawing order, these are listed in the order in which they are stacked up to make the map (we'll look at the other options later). Notice that each item has a small triangle to the left, which allows you to expand or collapse each item. Each layer can be expanded to view the symbology for that layer or collapsed to view just the layer name.

A key element of working with any mapping or design software is layer management. ArcPro lets you easily see your data layers, along with symbology and other details, in the **Contents** pane. The buttons underneath the **Search** bar change the way in which the data layers are displayed—by drawing order, file location, selectability, edit status, snapping, labeling, and chart content. Hover your mouse over each button to find out what it does. For now, make sure **Drawing Order** is selected:

Figure 2.3: Contents pane display settings

As we can see in, *Figure 2.2*, the **Contents** pane tree begins with **US Counties**, the name of this map. Underneath that the data layers that compose this map are listed. In this map, there is only one data layer so far, **US Counties**. Underneath the layer name is a colored square representing the symbol for that layer.

In complex maps, you may want to condense the **Contents** pane in order to see more information. You can reveal and hide the legend information (for example, the symbol properties, such as shading for areas or the shape used for the point) for a layer by clicking on the triangle next to the layer name. Click to reveal the legend; click again to hide it.

Across the top of the window, you'll see tabs labeled **US Counties** and **North America**. **US Counties** and **North America** are map frames, which are essentially individual maps made up of one or more map layers. In ArcMap, these were displayed as separate data frames within the same **Contents** pane. In the case of the project file you just opened, each tab contains one map. This will allow you to create and combine maps into a variety of layouts, which will be discussed later in the *Transitioning to the layout view* section. A **Map Frame** can comprise any of the data files (for example, **shapefiles**, **coverages**, and **rasters**) that can be added to ArcPro.

Click the **North America Map** tab to view it. When you are done, click the **US Counties Map** tab.

 The **US Counties** and **North America** maps have been projected using the North America Equidistant Conic projection. You will learn more about projections and how to set them in Chapter 7, *Understanding and Choosing Projections*.

In the ArcPro work environment, the ribbon and tools are anchored to the top of the program window. The tabs are context-sensitive and will change depending on what you are doing. You may notice some tabs appear when you click on certain things and disappear when you click away.

Take a few minutes to familiarize yourself with the menus and buttons located within the ArcPro window. To find out a button's name (and functionality), move the cursor over it. After a few seconds, the button command name will appear near the button and a brief description of the command will appear in a pop-up box near the tool. You may notice that some menu items and buttons are grayed out, or appear and disappear. Some menus and buttons are available only during specific situations.

By default, ArcPro does not display all of the available tools. To see a full list of available tools, click **Project|Options|Customize the Ribbon**.

Adding data to your map

Let's add a data layer to the **US Counties** map. Before we do, let's make sure ArcPro knows where your files are located. In the **Catalog** pane, expand **Folders** and see whether your data folder is shown.

If not, don't worry; your files are still where you left them! Right-click on **Folders** and select **Add Folder Connection** (don't see the **Catalog** pane? Click **View | Catalog | Catalog Pane**):

1. Browse to your folder and single-click it, then click **OK** (if you accidentally double-clicked, you will get a **This container is empty** message, and you will need to back up one level and single-click your folder):

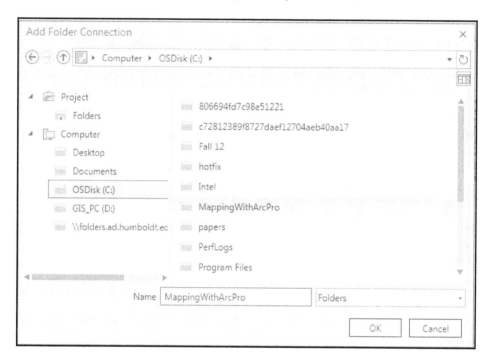

Figure 2.4: Add Folder Connection interface

You can create folder connections directly to a drive letter (for example, `C:\` or `D:\`) or a folder or sub-folder within that drive. However, you cannot see items in a parent folder or drive unless you are connected to it, so it's a good idea to connect to a top-level folder that contains all of your map projects and data (for example, `C:\ArcProProjects`) so you can see and browse all the folders without having to create a folder connection to each project folder you've created.

Once you're connected to your folder, you're ready to add data to your map.

2. Click the **Add Data** button to add a data layer:

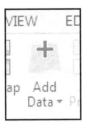

Figure 2.5 The Add Data button

3. The **Add Data** window will now appear. Browse to your newly connected folder:

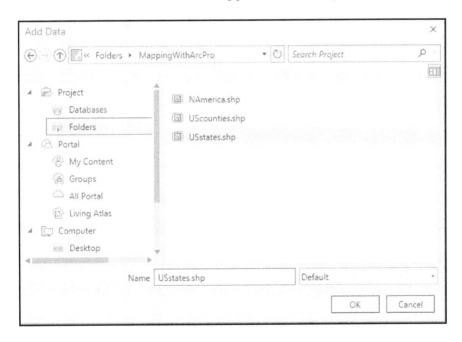

Figure 2.6: Files that can be added to your map layout

All three of the files have the `.shp` extension. These are **shapefiles**. Shapefiles contain vector data commonly used in GIS software. Vector data is data where points (either single points on a map, or vertices) are represented by coordinates. Common vector features include points, lines, and polygons.

Although only one filename appears with a `.shp` extension, shapefiles are actually collections of related files. When viewed in **File Explorer**, you will see all of the related files (as seen in the following figure). ArcGIS treats all of these files as a single object. For this reason, it is helpful to work with files in **Catalog**, rather than **File Explorer**, so none of the pieces get lost:

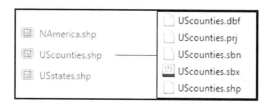

Figure 2.7: Each shapefile is a collection of related files

Let's add the **USstates** layer to the **US Counties** map. We saw this layer when we clicked on the **North America** map, but we want to use it in the **US Counties** map, also.

4. Add the `USstates.shp` file:

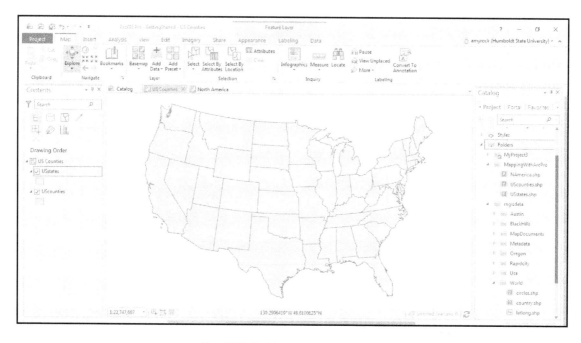

Figure 2.8: The Map View should display the states layer

Arranging layers

At first glance, it may appear that you only have one map layer displayed in the map view. This is because both the **Counties** and **State Outline** layers contain polygon features, and both files are currently using solid shading. When this happens, the polygons on top will obscure features underneath:

1. Deselect the checkbox next to **Counties** to turn off the layer. When you turn off the layer, you should see the **Illinois** outline layer. Turn the **Counties** layer back on.

   Note that beyond the layers in the **Contents** pane, it says **Drawing Order**. ArcGIS Pro renders your data from bottom to top, as if it were a stack of maps. The order in which the items appear in the **Contents** pane determines the order in which the layers are drawn. Some layers may be hidden beneath other layers. To change the order, click the layer name and drag the layer(s) up or down in the **Contents** pane. If you find you are unable to move your layers, make sure the first icon in the **Contents** pane is selected and that it says **Drawing Order**.

2. Click once on the **USstates** layer so that the layer name is highlighted. Now, drag the name so that it appears preceding the **UScounties** layer in the **Contents** pane. You will now see the outline with the counties being obscured:

Remember, if you have a lot of layers, you can collapse the legends so that you can see more layers on the screen.

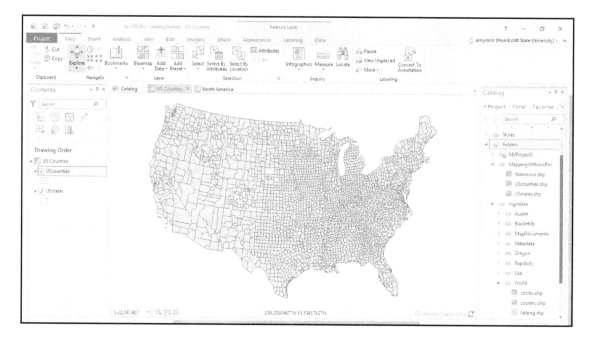

Figure 2.9: The Counties layer visible on top of the states layer

Renaming layers

When you add data to your map, it appears as a layer in the **Contents** pane. Sometimes the layer names do not clearly reflect the contents, as is the case with many public datasets. You can easily change the names to help you organize your content, without changing the file names. Let's change the layer names in the **Contents** pane to something that makes more sense for our project:

1. Right-click once on **UScounties**. A context menu will now appear. Select **Properties** (the last item in the menu).

2. Select the **General** tab. In the **Layer Name** box, change the name of the layer from **UScounties** to Counties. Change the name of **USstates** to State Outline. Note that this does not affect your filenames. Look at the files in your **Catalog** pane (at right), and you'll see that this does not change the names of the files in your folder.

   In ArcGIS Pro, there is frequently more than one way to do something. In this case, we could also change the layer name by slowly double-clicking the layer name (with a slight pause in between) and then typing the new name when it appears editable. The **Properties** window is a great place to perform lots of other tasks, in addition to renaming layers.

3. Before you do anything else, it is a good idea to save your project. Click the **Save** button. If you wish to save your project under a different name, click **File|Save As...**.When working on map projects, get into the habit of saving your work often!

Working in the Map View

Map View allows us to compose maps individually. As we have just seen, the information viewable in the map view is controlled by the **Contents** pane. We can set visibility and stack layers, as well as update layer names to legend-friendly labels.

Symbolizing layers

For this map, we want the state boundaries to serve as outlines for the counties, so if it's not already on top, bring the **State Outline** layer to the top of the **Drawing Order**.

Beneath each of the map layers in the **Contents** pane is the legend for that layer. At this point, each layer has only a single symbol:

1. Click once on the colored box for **State Outline** in the **Contents** pane to reveal the **Symbology** pane. The **Symbology** pane is where you set the display characteristics of map features:

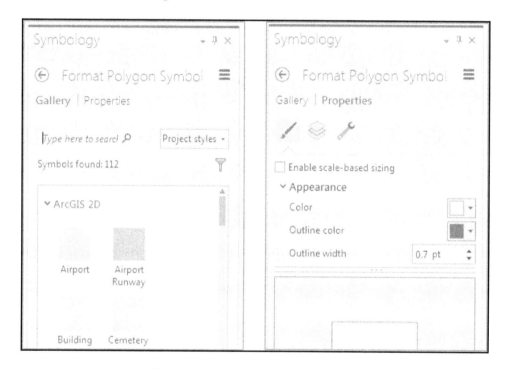

Figure 2.10: The Symbology pane, and Gallery and Properties tabs

We want to see both the state boundaries and the counties, so let's change the properties of the **States** symbol to display just the outline. Switch to **Properties** on this pane if it is not already there.

2. Set the **Fill Color** to **No Color**. Set the **Outline color** to Black. The preview at the bottom of the pane will update. Click **Apply** to update the map with these changes.

Let's make one change, to make the state boundaries stand out from the county boundaries. Right now, the line thickness **Outline width**) is **0.7 pt**, the same as in the **Counties** layer. If we leave it at this width, the only distinction from the county boundaries is that it may be slightly darker, which might be difficult to determine. Let's change that.

3. Change the thickness to 2 by clicking the up arrow or typing 2 in the box to the right of the **Outline width** box. Click **Apply** to update the map.
    The outline will now appear much thicker, perhaps even too thick. As you gain familiarity with the software, you'll get a sense of how thick lineweights should be, but know that they may appear slightly different on the screen than they will when printed. In fact, lines in particular appear thicker in the **Map View** than they do in **Layout View**.

4. If the **Symbology** pane is still open, click on the **Counties** symbol; otherwise, repeat the previous steps to open the pane for the **Counties** layer. Change the **Fill Color** to White. Leave the **Outline color** and width for the moment.

5. Click **Apply** to update the map and close the **Properties** window. Your map should now resemble the **US Counties** map shown in the following section.

Adding a little something extra

For cartographic purposes, we often add layers to the map for purely aesthetic reasons. For example, we might add in a **State Outline** twice—once as a crisp border, and once as a drop shadow. Let's create a simulated drop shadow for our **Counties** map:

1. Right-click on the **State Outline** layer and select **Copy**.
2. Right-click on the **Map Frame** name (**US Counties**) and select **Paste**. You now have a second **State Outline** layer (make sure that this does not create an extra copy of the file in your folder; it merely adds the same file to your map for the second time).
3. Drag this layer to the bottom of the **Drawing Order** and change its name to **Drop Shadow**.

4. Change the outline to gray 30% and **4 pt**, and click **Apply**:

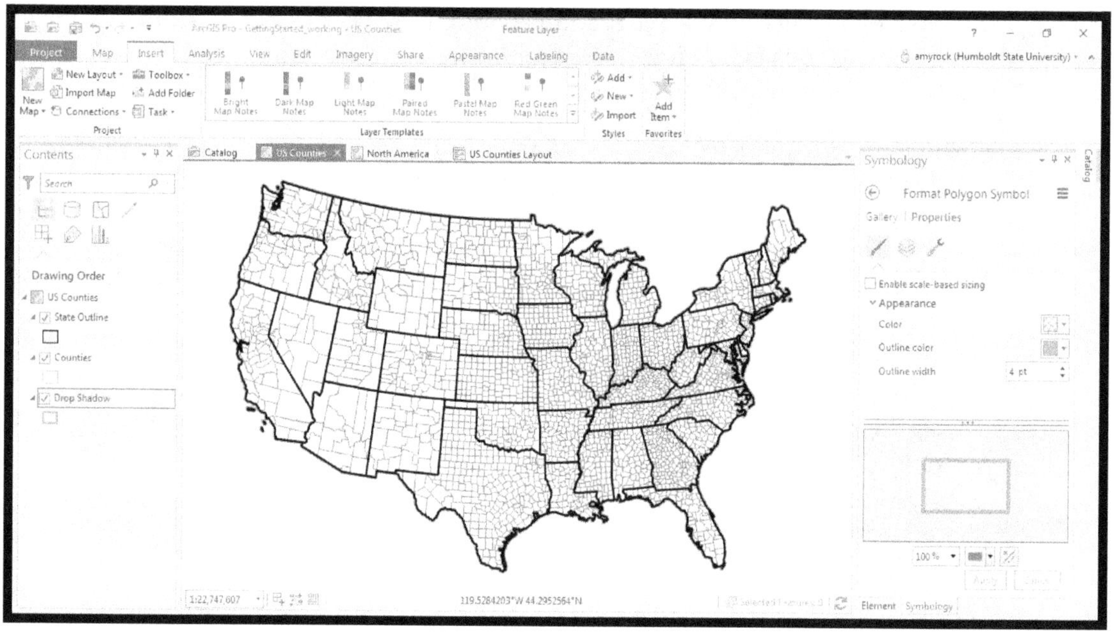

Figure 2.11: The US Counties map

Symbolizing multiple values

Sometimes, we want to be able to symbolize features in a layer differently. We'll do this in more detail in future chapters, but for now, we just want to symbolize the United States so that it will stand out against the other countries for a locator map:

1. Switch to the **North America Map** tab. This is going to become our locator map in the final layout. It may look a little strange right now, but we'll fix that.

2. As we did with the **US Counties** map, let's rename the map layer to something more meaningful. Since we're going to be zooming in to focus on **North America**, name it **North America**. In this map, you will be shading the United States a medium-gray color, while leaving the other states white. This step is a bit more complicated than the previous step, as opening the **Symbology** from the **Contents** pane changes the symbol properties for all symbols.

3. If the **Symbology** pane is still open, click on the **Cntry_NAmerica** layer name. Otherwise, click the symbol first to open the pane, then click the layer name to launch the **Symbology** pane to a different function than previously. (You can also reach this option by clicking the back arrow at the top of the pane.)

4. In the **Symbology** drop-down menu, select **Unique Values**.

5. Change the value field to **CNTRY_NAME**. Since this is a long list, you'll get a message that there are more than 100 unique values. Select **No**, since we don't want to generate the full list of unique values at this time:

Figure 2.12: Generating unique values

At the bottom of the pane, a partial list of countries appears.

6. Click the **More** button and select **Remove all**. This will clear out the list and leave only the **<all other values>** option.

7. Click the plus symbol (**+**) over this pane (or click **More** again) to **Add values**. The pane will switch to the list of values. You may see the message about adding all values again; say **Yes** this time.

8. Scroll to the **United States** and select it by clicking on it once, and click the **OK** button:

Figure 2.13: Selecting a value from the list

Your **Symbology** window will now contain **<all other values>** and the **United States**:

9. Click the box next to **United States** to open the **Symbology**. Change the **Fill Color** to gray 50% (hover the mouse over a color for a second or two, and the color name will appear in a pop-up box) and the **Outline color** to Black. Click **Apply** to commit changes and click the back button at the top of the pane to return to the previous screen.

10. Repeat this step for **<all other values>,** but set the **Fill Color** to gray 10% and the **Outline color** to Black.

    Close the **Symbology** pane. Your map should appear as follows:

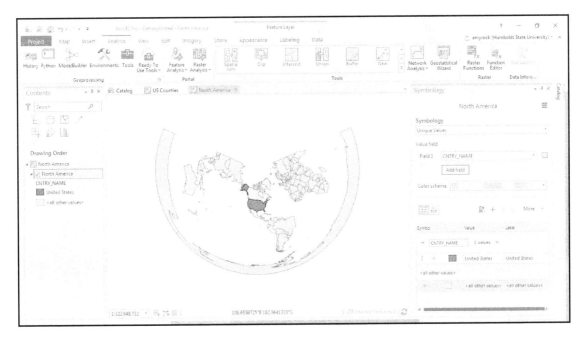

Figure 2.14: The North America map

Setting bookmarks

Since we are setting this up as a locator map for our **US Counties** map, we will focus on **North America**. To zoom into our desired area, hold the *Shift* key and move the mouse over the **Map View**. Notice that your cursor changes to a magnifying glass. Click and drag a box around **North America** to zoom in.

The **Map** tab on the ribbon contains several other tools for zooming and panning around the map. In the **Navigate** section, you'll find the **Explore** button, which has several drop-down options, but which, when active, allows you to pan around the map with the hand icon. There are a number of options for zooming in and out on your map:

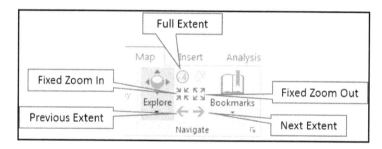

Figure 2.15: Zoom tools

Let's have a look at each of the icons in detail:

- **Full Extent**: This icon zooms to the full extent of all data layers in the map.
- **Previous Extent**: This icon zooms back to your previous extent.
- **Next Extent**: This icon should remain grayed out until after you've used the **Previous Extent** tool. Once it's active, you can hop back and forth between zoom levels.

You can also zoom in and out on your map incrementally by using the **Fixed Zoom In** and **Fixed Zoom Out** buttons. The *Shift*-Zoom feature works well when you have a specific extent to which you want to zoom, as in this case.

Your map should now look something like this:

Figure 2.16: Map zoomed to North America

This is a common level at which we want to view our data, and also the extent we'll display as our locator map when we move to the **Layout View**. To make sure we can easily come back to this same extent, we'll set a **Bookmark**.

If you've been experimenting with the zoom and pan tools, return to the extent shown in preceding figure:

1. Click the **Bookmark** icon and select **New Bookmark.**
2. Name your bookmark North America and click **OK**.
3. Now, when you click **Bookmarks**, you will see your new bookmark with a thumbnail for handy reference.
4. Test it out! Click the **Full Extent** button and zoom out to the whole world again.
5. Then, click **Bookmarks** and select your bookmark.

Bookmarks are a great way to keep track of areas for your final map layout, but also for checking details or creating multiple layout options from a single map. You can create as many bookmarks as you like for each map.

Transitioning to the Layout View

When you create a map for printing or digital publication, you work in the **Layout View**. Now that we've got our individual maps symbolized and ready to go, it's time to assemble a layout:

1. Click **Insert|New Layout** to add a layout to your project. Select letter-size paper from the **ANSI Landscape** category as your size and orientation. You now have a virtual page, a page that allows you to organize all the map elements before printing.

2. To add a map to your layout, click the **Map Frame** button on the ribbon. From the drop-down menu, select the **Default** map under **US Counties**. This will give you a full-page frame of your **Counties** map.

3. Click the **Map Frame** button again to add the **North America** map. This time, select the **North America Bookmark** you made to add a quarter-page frame (since we'll be reducing this anyway, it's easier to start with a smaller frame than to completely overlap the previous frame). If you picked the wrong one, just delete it and try again. Your maps are still dynamically connected to their original map frames. You can make changes to the maps in either the **Map** tab or the **Layout** tab, and both will be updated. In the **Contents** pane, you'll see each **Map Frame** listed in the collapsed form. As in **Map View**, you can expand and collapse these by clicking on the small triangle to the left of each item. You can also lock a **Map Frame** to prevent accidental changes while working on other parts of the layout:

When a **Map Frame** is locked in the **Contents** pane, you cannot select or make changes to that item. If you find you are unable to select a frame when working with your layout, verify that it is unlocked in the **Contents** pane.

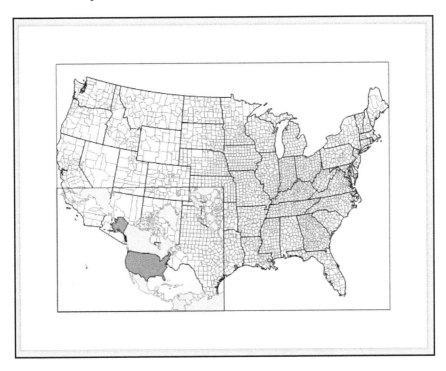

Figure 2.17: The data frames are displayed overlapped on the page

Page setup

Since you chose this format when setting your layout, your map has a landscape orientation (the long edge is horizontal). You will keep this orientation for this map layout, but for future reference, this can be changed in the **Layout Properties**:

1. Right-click the virtual page outside of any selected data frames and click **Properties**. Select **Page Setup** (you can also access this from the **Page Setup** section of the layout ribbon). Verify your page size and other settings here:

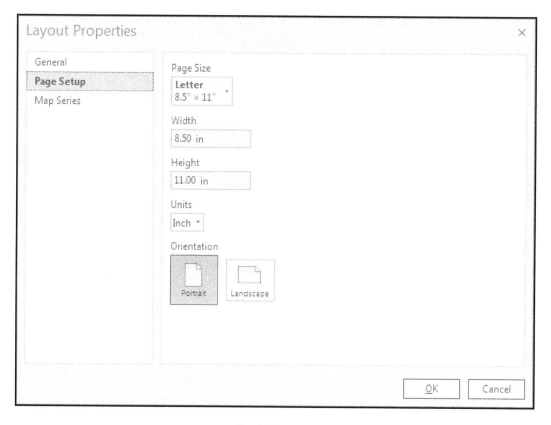

Figure 2.18: Page setup

While we're here, let's update the name of our layout:

2. In **Layout Properties**, select **General** on the left. Change the **Name** to US Counties Layout. Click **OK** and note that the name updates on the tab at the top of the layout window.

Printer margins are not visible in ArcPro, but be aware that most printers cannot print all the way to the edges of the page. To make sure you stay within the printable area, add guides to your page by right-clicking on the ruler and selecting **Add Guides...** (make sure to select the one with the ...). Select **both** to place around all margins. Under **Placement**, select **Offset from edge** and set the **Margin** to **0.25 in**, which is suitable for most printers.

Working with map frames

Notice that in the **Layout View**, the maps overlap with no sense of priority. The **Counties** map appears in the center of the layout, and the **North America** locator is pinned to the lower-left corner. For now, let's rename the map frames for clarity:

1. Select the **Counties** map by clicking on it (make sure you have not locked your map frames):

When an item in the layout is selected, you'll see boxes at the corners and midpoints. These boxes (called handles) allow you to resize the frame. Clicking the frame between the handles allows you to move it. Click anywhere outside the frame to deselect it.

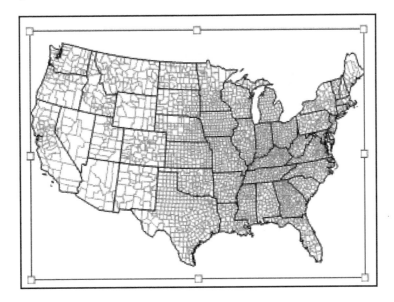

Figure 2.19: A selected item in the layout

2. Using the same technique we used for the map layers, rename your **US Counties** map frame to US Counties.

3. Repeat this process for the **North America** map frame and name it Locator Map. Also, notice how both maps are drawn with a black line around them. By default, ArcPro draws a **neatline** around your map frames.

4. Switch to the **Map Frame** tab, which has now appeared on the ribbon, to access formatting choices for this frame. In the **Current Selection** drop-down menu at the top-left corner, select **Border**. Remove the neatline by selecting **No Color** in the **Line** drop-down:

Figure 2.20: The Map Frame tab allows you to change the outline, fill, and drop shadow properties for the data frame

5. To keep the **Locator Map** from looking like islands off the coast of the US, we'll leave the border on it, but change it to a medium gray. Repeat the preceding steps and select gray 50% as the line color.

Locator maps are an important map element when you need to place your data in larger geographical context to help your map reader understand the scope or location of the map. While important, this is still secondary or tertiary information, so locator maps should be small and tucked away from the visual center in a way that works with the overall balance of the map.

Let's resize and reposition this data frame:

1. Select the **Locator Map**. Verify that the **Map Frame** is unlocked.

2. Make sure the **Current Selection** is set to **Map Frame**. Set the **Size** and **Position** at the right end of the ribbon. Make the **Width 2.5 in** and the **Height 2 in**. Press *Enter* or click in another field to register your changes:

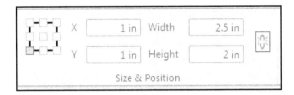

Figure 2.21: In addition to specifying the data frame dimensions, you can place it in a specific location on the page

3. Let's tuck the **Locator Map** in the lower left-hand corner of the layout, for balance. Drag the frame to the corner and leave a gap between the **Map Frame** and the print margins (faint gray lines). Try to make the gaps at the left and at the bottom the same size.

Creating a map output

Now that we've fixed the overlap problem, it's time to add the remaining map elements and finish our map. Regardless of whether you are designing for print or screen, a good map contains a title, north arrow, scale bar, and credits, which include the author name, date, source, and projection information. We'll also add a neatline to give a finished look to our map.

First, let's add a neatline to the layout. Neatlines are also sometimes referred to as borders, and are used to frame objects in a map layout for style or clarity. Too many neatlines can result in clutter, so for now, we'll just create a neatline around the entire map layout:

1. Click **Insert|Rectangle**.
2. Click and drag a box around the map near the margins. If you added guides beyond, you will see it snap to those if you stay close to them. The guides are always on top, so they may obscure some of your neatlines. To verify what's underneath, right-click outside the virtual page and uncheck guides. Repeat and check them again to restore them.
3. The **Format** tab will appear, allowing you to format your neatline.
4. Set the **Line fill** to Black and the **Width** to **2 pt**.
5. Make sure the **Fill** is set to **No Color**.

Since this is a common neatline style, there is also a template for this. From the **Insert** tab, select the drop-down on the square to the left of the rectangle tool and scroll down to **Common**. You'll see a **Black Outline** available in **1 pt** and **2 pt** options.

Note that your rectangle is now added as an object in your **Contents** pane, allowing you to easily move it to the back. Let's do that now:

1. Select the **Rectangle** in the **Contents** pane.
2. Rename it to `Neatline` and drag it to the bottom of the **Drawing Order**.

Adding map elements

An important element in any map is an understanding of scale, to provide readers with a sense of the scope of the map, as well as provide a measurement tool if needed. We have created maps at two different scales, but it is generally not necessary to provide a scale for locator maps, so we'll just create one for the more detailed **US Counties** map. The scale bar tool generates a scale for whichever map frame is selected, but don't worry if you've accidentally started the process with the wrong frame selected, as ArcGIS Pro makes it easy to switch frames after the scale bar is inserted.

To make sure you are inserting the scale bar for the correct map, click on the **US Counties** frame to select it:

1. Click **Insert | Scale Bar**. Under the imperial section (feet and miles), select **Alternating Scale Bar 1**. Drag it to the bottom of the map so you can see it clearly, then right-click and select **Properties**. First, verify that you have it set for the correct map. Next to **Map Frame**, **US Counties** should be selected:

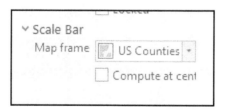

Figure 2.22: Verifying the Scale Bar is set to the correct map frame

2. Under the **Scale Bar** tab in the ribbon, select **Design** and set the following:

- **Resize behavior: Adjust Width**
- **Division value: 50 mi**
- **Number of divisions: 5**
- **Number of subdivisions: 2**
- **Units: Miles**

- **Label position**: Your choice

Scale bars should generally be set to end at -50 or -00 values. Ending a **Scale Bar** at a value not divisible by five is never advisable. If the size of the **Scale Bar** is not appropriate for your map, adjust the number of divisions, or set **Resize Behavior** to **Adjust Division Value** and use the handles to resize, adjusting until the values meet the criteria mentioned earlier.

3. To soften the weight of this very heavy looking element, switch to the **Format** tab and set the following using the **Current Selection** drop-down to change components:

- **Scale Bar**:
    - **Line**: 70% gray
    - **Width**: 0.5 pt
    - **Font**: Your choice, **Color**: 70% gray
- Symbol 1:
    - **Fill**: 70% gray
    - **Line**: 70% gray
    - **Width**: 0.5 pt

Place the **Scale Bar** in the bottom-center portion of the map of the layout (make sure it is inside the neatline), lined up with the bottom of the **Locator Map**. You should see dotted lines appear as you snap to this alignment, or you can add another guide to your ruler. If you do not see the rulers in the display, right-click on the virtual page and make sure **Rulers** is checked. Check your **Scale Bar** to make sure the length makes sense for your map. If you accidentally selected the wrong frame in the first step, just go back to the **Properties** and select the correct map frame. Next, you will add a north arrow:

1. Click **Insert | North Arrow**. Select **ArcGIS North 4** and it will appear in the center of the map. Place the **North Arrow** in the lower-right, roughly centered in the white space between the map and the **Scale Bar**. Try to center it as best as possible in this space.

2. As with the **Scale Bar**, make sure the **North Arrow** is aligned to the **US Counties** map. Verify this on the **Design** tab on the ribbon, or the **Format North Arrow** pane at the right. Leave the **Type** at **True North** for now, we'll discuss this more in Chapter 7, *Understanding and Choosing Projections*:

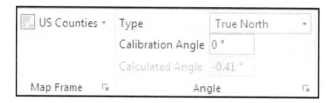

Figure 2.23: Verifying North Arrow is set to correct map frame

Notice these elements also appear in the **Drawing Order** and can be renamed and reorganized. Be careful not to hide your map elements underneath your map!

Now you will add text elements to the map; the first will be the map title:

1. Click **Insert | Text** and click near the top of the map. A text element will appear where you click.
2. Replace **Text** with **US Counties**. The **Format** tab and pane will reappear. Highlight all of the text, or click on the map and click on your text to select it for modification.
3. With the title selected (indicated by the handles), change the font to **Times New Roman**; make the font size **48 pt** and make the title **Bold**. You probably noticed that the title and map were crowded together. Generally, you want the title balanced in the available white space at the top. This may vary depending on your layout. For now, we'll center it over the map
4. With the title selected, move it with the mouse, or use the *Ctrl* + arrow keys on the keyboard to nudge the title. Move it until you have the same-sized gaps over and under the title. Use the dotted snapping guides that appear to help you.
5. Use **Insert | Text** again to place the final elements. Do one at a time, moving the text element to its correction location before doing the next item, so you have a clear sense of where everything needs to be placed.
6. For the first text element, type **Projection: North America Equidistant Conic**. Move this item to the bottom of the map, centered underneath the scale bar. Change the font to **Arial, 8 pt**. Do not make this text bold. Align it with the bottom edge of your **Locator Map**.

It's important to credit your source data, and also to include information on who made the map and when, as this helps others determine the timeliness and relevance of your map:

1. Add your map credits individually along the bottom of the map under the **Scale Bar** (**8 point**, **Arial**):

```
Your name
   Today's date
   Source: Esri
```

2. Align it in the lower-right corner of the map, lined up with the bottom of the **Locator**. Try to balance the space between it and the neatline to be the same size as the space between the locator and the left side of the neatline.

3. To right-justify this text so it lines up neatly with the right corner of the neatline, use the **Format Text** pane, which also appears when you select text. Change to **Text Symbol** and scroll down to **Position**. Set the **Horizontal alignment** to right-justify and click **Apply:**

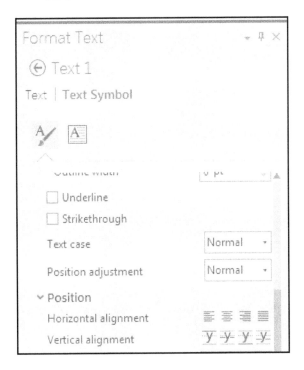

Figure 2.24: Setting text alignment

The final map should look something like the following:

Figure 2.25: Final map layout, based on this tutorial

Sharing your map

By default, ArcPro creates your map in the **Red**, **Green**, **Blue** (**RGB**) color model, which is designed for display on a screen. We'll discuss color models in more detail in Chapter 5, *Picking Colors with Confidence*, but for now, let's set this to **Cyan**, **Magenta**, **Yellow**, and **Black** or **Key** (**CMYK**) to prepare our map for a print output:

1. Right-click outside the virtual page and select **Properties**.
2. In general, set the **Color Model** to **CMYK** and click **OK**.
   Since our map is designed in black and white, you probably won't notice much difference on the screen, but your printer will know the difference, and it will give you cleaner blacks and grays on this setting. If you've got a printer set up on your computer, go ahead and print out a copy of your new map.
3. On the **Share** tab, select **Layout** in the **Print** section. This will open the print dialog box, and you can select your printer and set the number of copies and so on from here.

No printer? No worries. You can create a PDF to print out later by clicking **Layout** in the **Export** section. The default output should be PDF at 300 dpi (set to this if otherwise), so just browse to your folder, name your file, and click **Export**.

We'll get more into the specifics of designing for the screen in later chapters, but if you want to share this on a web page, PowerPoint presentation, or another digital platform, set the **Color Model** back to **RGB** and use **Export Layout** to create a PNG file which is compatible with most applications.

Practice on your own

Did you notice that Alaska and Hawaii were missing? Practice on your own by creating new map frames for each with the Alaska and Hawaii counties, symbolizing and setting bookmarks, then bringing them into your layout and arranging them.

Summary

In this chapter, we gained familiarity with the ArcGIS Pro interface, including working with panes and the ribbon. We worked with data layers in the **Contents** pane, adding, organizing, and renaming them, and learned how to change the basic symbolization for a layer. We then learned to represent some features differently and add copies of existing layers to enhance the look of the map. We spent some time in the **Map View**, then switched to the **Layout View** to work with map frames and prepare a final output for print or screen.

In the next chapter, we'll take an in-depth look at the overall framework of maps, learning the principles of design and layout that improve the map's communication and make maps irresistible.

3
Organizing the Page Structure

Good page composition is as important as good map data. If your map is not well designed, information may not be clearly communicated, or worse, no one may bother to look at your map. In this chapter, we're going to talk about all of the pieces that need to come together to make a great map. We'll look at some ways to make them less standardized and fit better with the language of your map.

In this chapter, we will cover the following topics:

- Beginning the mapping process
- Achieving good design
- Working with multiple data frames

Beginning the mapping process

The main goal of a map is to facilitate the transfer of knowledge between the map author and reader. It's important to communicate important information, but we must also attract and retain the viewer's interest. After all, if no one looks at your map, your information doesn't get communicated at all! The design of your map, like a well-articulated argument, can either support or hinder your message.

The **design** is a process, with specific strategies and benchmarks to help us achieve clear communication. Bad design is usually easy to spot—we can quickly point to why or how something isn't working. Good design can be harder to identify. If all the elements are working together as they should, everything is seamless.

In mapping, we work with the trinity of balance, harmony, and unity. **Balance** is the art of placing elements around the page so that they don't draw the eye unnaturally to one side or the other. While symmetry is seldom possible (particularly with maps, since we have no control over the shape of an area), we can still achieve balance through careful planning.

Unity means that the map elements all look like they belong together, rather than loosely assembled from a variety of sources. This improves comprehension and is a clear sign of professionalism. This may extend beyond a single map to a map series, and be required to coordinate with the design of other materials, such as a report or corporate branding.

Finally, harmony is the most difficult to quantify. In a visually harmonious map, the message is clear, and the map looks less like it was assembled and more like it magically appeared fully developed. All the pieces are working together to lead the map reader through the information in a logical way, with map elements forming the supporting cast rather than trying to be the stars of the show.

Achieving good design

A key stage in developing a good design is the compilation process. Many cartographers still sketch out a layout on paper before starting, but others prefer to sketch digitally, which is essentially what you're doing in this chapter. In the compilation sheet, you'll add placeholders for the parts of your map to create a digital sketch, and determine size and placement to achieve balance, harmony, and unity.

Since few geographic features are symmetrical, we can't just drop it in the center of the page and consider it done. Even if the map is bounded into a nice square by a neatline, the shape of the subject area is still going to impact how it's placed within that space, and perhaps whether other map elements go on top of that square, or outside of it.

Let's start by looking at some of the ways in which balance is established (or disturbed) by the component parts of our map. Visual balance is affected by the relative weight of the symbols, and the location of the elements with respect to each other and the visual center of the map. The **Visual Center** of the page is where our eyes are drawn first, and is different than the actual, or **Geometric Center**. If you were to draw lines connecting the corners of the page, these lines would intersect at the geometric center. The visual center is about 5% beyond that, so it varies depending on the size and orientation of your page as shown in the following figure:

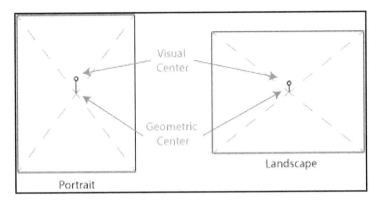

Figure 3.1: Locating the visual center of a page

Not only do our eyes gravitate to a point slightly over the geometric center, but they also travel around the page in very specific ways. For those of us who read predominantly in languages written left to right, our eyes have developed a natural tendency to scan a page from the upper-left to the lower-right. While reading, we scan in a Z motion, across a line, down to the start of the next, and so forth. If the page is not covered in words, but rather in graphics, as with a map, we tend to shortcut that Z shape and take a more direct diagonal from upper-left to lower-right. However, our eyes will hang up on that visual center, the **Focus**, resulting in an imperfect vector across the page. The area around that is called the **Field**, and our eyes will take in that information as our attention is caught by the focus. The **Fringe** is everything else, and as our eyes leave the center, they will continue to dip to the lower-right corner as shown in the following figure. However, if there happens to be something in the upper-right corner that looks interesting, we will detour from that path:

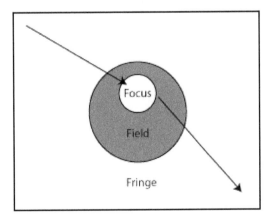

Figure 3.2: Natural eye movement across a page

In designing the map page, we want to work with this natural focus of attention—where our eyes settle first, and how they move naturally across a page. The key focus of the map needs to be at the visual center, and the upper-right corner should be low on distractions.

Let's take a look at our counties map from the Chapter 2, *Getting Started in ArcGIS Pro*. Since this is a compilation sheet and not a final map, we can use placeholders for the other elements that will go in this map. In this example, as seen in the following figure, map elements are tucked around the edges of the map, as they should be, but with no clear sense of organization. Our eyes are bouncing around looking at all the map elements, with no real reward, getting pulled away from the main message:

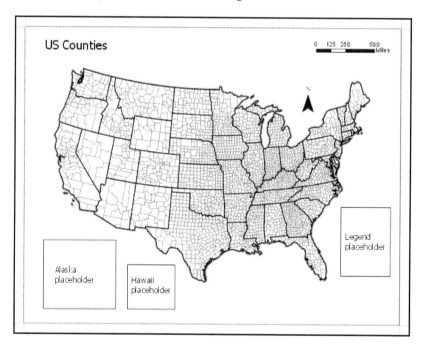

Figure 3.3: Poor placement of map elements

Did you get sucked into spending time in the upper-right corner? That's not what we want. Now, look at what happens when we declutter that space, line things up a bit, and bring the title into more prominence:

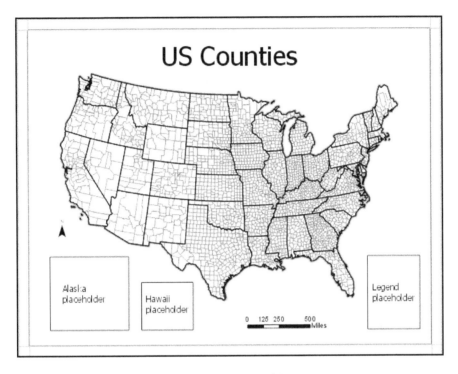

Figure 3.4: Improved organization of elements

The eye is not drawn to the upper-right; it hovers around the center of the map, and can then drop-down through natural movement to find the rest of the elements. It is more balanced, resting on a stable base of elements, and it's easier for the eye to spend time in the main part of the map without getting distracted.

Finding balance

Balancing elements on the page comes down to two key factors—weight and position. The weight of elements refers to its tendency to draw the eye away from the visual center of the page. Position, of course, means placement relative to the focus or field. Items that are located in the fringe, in particular, the right side or upper half, are extremely likely to distract the view from the focal point. Centrally located items can often be viewed with little or no eye movement away from the center, and because of our left to right reading habits, the left side and the lower half are typically ignored by the viewer until they are done with the items in the center. Regular and compact shapes appear heavier than irregular or diffuse shapes. Isolated items draw the eye more than members of a group, and large elements more so than small.

The following table is a relative weight of elements on a page:

More weight	Less weight
Peripherally located (fringe) Upper half Right side Isolated elements Large elements Red elements Regular shapes Compact shapes Vertically oriented	Centrally located (field) Lower half Left side Elements in groups Small elements Blue elements Irregular shapes Diffuse shapes Horizontally oriented

Some of these are easy to control, by changing the color, or making line weights or fonts thinner, while others are more difficult. Many of these weight factors are also related to the position on the page. We can't shift the islands in an archipelago to make them suit our need for weight in the center of the page, but we can adjust the elements around them to make the islands appear to be the heaviest part of the map.

Here's an example using *Hawaii*. The islands themselves are positioned nicely along the natural eye path, but they don't stand out as well as they should. They are also naturally off-balance, most of the weight is in the lower-right corner. The sparseness of actual land means that most of the map, and all of the elements, are located in the fringe:

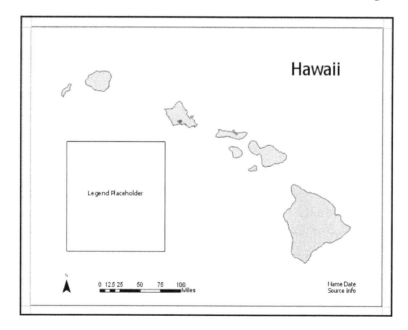

Figure 3.5: Hawaii with equally weighted elements

Now, let's change the weight of a few things. Even though the title is heavy and in the upper-right corner, it's a single word, so it's a quick glance and back to the map, unlike our complex map elements from before. The islands are brought into prominence with a bold outline, and the map elements are softened, making them less attention-grabbing. Without changing the position of any elements, the tracking is made easier by drawing attention to the important parts of the map as shown in the following figure:

Figure 3.6: Hawaii with re-weighted elements

Lessening the weight of the elements also allows us to put more stuff in the lower-left part of the map, where there is plenty of room, without bogging the whole thing down. We still have a nice stable platform of aligned elements along the bottom, and the bold title balances the lower-left cluster, and lifts the eye up, helping to keep it from settling into the largest island.

While we can't change the geography of our map location, we can choose where everything else is placed. We've already decided that we need to have the main focus of the map located around the visual center, but how do we place everything else? Sometimes, as with Hawaii, the shape of the map determines where elements should go. The arrangement of islands almost exactly fits the path along which the eye tracks naturally. Sometimes we have more freedom to choose, and sometimes the geography runs counter to the natural eye path, from lower-left to upper-right, and we have to add weight on the left side of the page just to balance it. When we are measuring balance, we want to compare left to right, and top to bottom. Since we know perfect symmetry is seldom possible, how do we achieve this?

Unfortunately, there's no perfect formula, and developing a keen sense of balance comes only with practice. However, a good place to start is by adding grid lines to your layout to divide your page into left/right and top/bottom. The following figure shows a page divided into quarters, with a third guide added to indicate the visual center. We want to concentrate the reader's attention here, but we may shift slightly off towards left or right to add visual interest and make way for a legend, if it is sizeable and the shape of the geography lends itself. Recall that the upper-right is the most distracting place to put elements, and the lower-left the least. We should focus on limiting that top-right to title or map pieces, and the lower-left can carry the weight of a large block of text or a heavy legend:

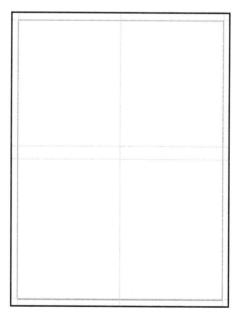

Figure 3.7: Page guides for determining balance

That said, a lot of this depends on the overall density of the map subject. In, *Figure 3.6*, our geography is somewhat sparse, which restricts us to light weights or sparse distribution for everything else. Sometimes, our map fills the **Map Frame**, and we have to move elements outside the frame completely, as with this layout for a section of Manhattan:

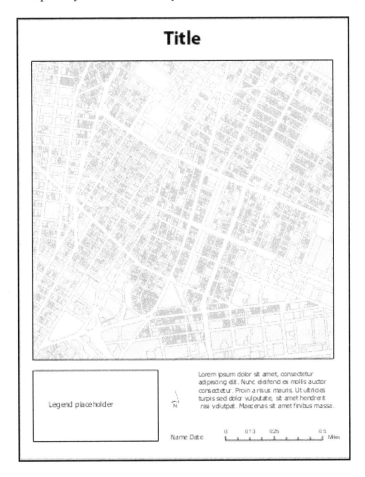

Figure 3.8: The sample layout with all elements outside the map frame

In this case, a lot of the balance is managed by the **Map Frame** itself, and we only have to worry about balancing the elements across the bottom. This is also a handy strategy if you're building a map series with a lot of different maps that make homogenous element placement difficult.

Let's practice with a slightly more complicated area. We already know that we can use guides in **Layout View** to help you find print margins, but we can also use them to help place elements and establish balance, as shown in, *Figure 3.7*:

1. Open the compilation project and insert a **New Layout**. Select **Letter** from the **ANSI Portrait** category as your size and orientation.
2. First, let's add in our page margins. Right-click on the ruler and select **Add Guides...**.
3. Select **Both** to place around all margins. Under **Placement**, select **Offset from edge** and set the **Margin** to **0.25** inches, which is suitable for most printers.
4. Now, let's create a placement grid. Right-click on the top ruler and select **Add Guides...**. By selecting this on the top ruler, the selection defaults to **Vertical**. Our paper size is 8 ½ inches x 11 inches, so let's add a vertical guide at **4.25** inches. Select **Single location**, and set **Position** to **4.25** inches.
5. Right-click on the ruler on the left to set a horizontal guide at a single location at **5.5** inches.
6. Let's add one more for the visual center. Our page height is 11 inches, so 5% is just over half an inch. Set a horizontal guide at **6** inches (half the page height plus half an inch). Your page should now look like, *Figure 3.7*.
7. From the **Insert** tab, select **Map Frame**, and add the **NZ bookmark**. Use the handles to stretch the **Map Frame**, and snap it to your print margins.
8. Add in a **Scale Bar** and **North Arrow**, and a title. Since we don't yet know the subject of this map, we'll call it something really imaginative, like **New Zealand**. Remember that your title is in the second tier of information, so it should be nice and large.
9. Add some map credits—name, date, and source information. Remember this is tertiary stuff, so no matter how proud you are of a map, it should be pretty small text, generally around 8 pt font.
10. To make a legend placeholder, add a **Rectangle** from the **Insert** tab. Click and drag a box somewhere in the empty space on your map. I added a small piece of text to mine to keep track of what it represents, but that's up to you.

Now we have a little dilemma—do we put it over or under the land mass? We know that things on the left are lighter than things on the right, but things on the top are heavier than the bottom. So, what's the answer? It depends on what else is happening with the map. First, how many legend items will you have? If it's only one or two, that changes the weight of the legend.

It might fit right at the visual center, to the left of the islands. If it's a big, heavy legend, the best place is probably the lower-right, and you can balance it out by changing the title weight and position, maybe shifting the island north a little. What else is going on this map? Are you labeling the water bodies? What about the islands? Here are a few examples:

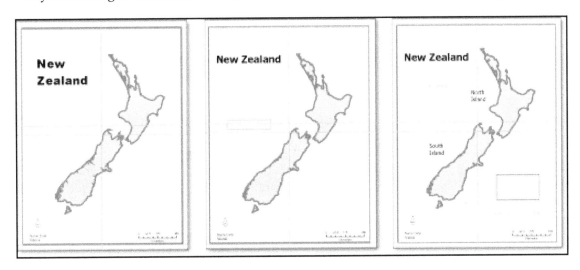

Figure 3.9: Experimenting with balance

Experiment with your layout—remember that there is no absolute right way to do it, just try to achieve an overall sense of balance. Also remember that whitespace is a good thing, and you don't have to fill up every square inch of paper.

Establishing harmony

Harmony refers to how well the elements work together. The establishment of harmony is related to balance but involves the development of a good visual hierarchy. Which elements need to be read first, or made to stand out? Which elements need to be subdued for clarity or lack of importance? Is your north arrow vying for attention with your subject material? Is the legend overpowering the title? To build hierarchy, we need to organize our map elements into three principal categories—primary, secondary, and tertiary information.

The primary information is limited to the key information we are trying to communicate, the map itself. Secondary information includes the title and the legend. If the map is going into a report with a caption, the title might be omitted, in which case the legend is the only piece of secondary information. Everything else is considered tertiary information—the scale bar, the directional indicator, notes and credits, logos, all of it. The following figure demonstrates the sequence in which the map items should get the attention of the reader.

 This is not the same thing as the order in which they appear on the actual map.

We want our reader to see **The Map** first, then the **Title** and **Legend** to help frame context. The rest of the information is just there for reference—the fine print, if you will. If the reader wants to measure something, they'll hunt out the scale bar; if they want to know which way is north, they'll look for the arrow, but generally they'll assume north is at the top of the page (exception to this is if north is not up then you'll need to place a tiny bit more emphasis on the directional indicator, but don't get carried away):

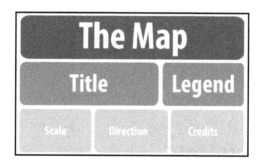

Figure 3.10: Map hierarchy

Tying this back to what we have learned about balance, placing tertiary information in the focus or the field is never a good idea.

In a previous example of the **US Counties** shown in, *Figure 3.4*, all of the elements had roughly the same weight, so there wasn't any real sense of what was important. Here's the same map, with the weights changed:

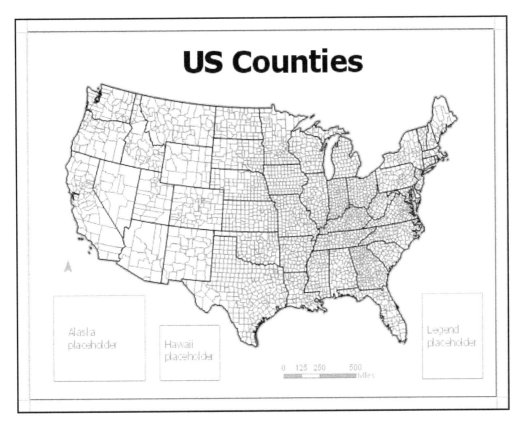

Figure 3.11: Building hierarchy

This time, the map pops out a little more prominently, as does the title. The legend is about at the same level as the two inset maps, and the other elements are less prominent.

This hierarchy development also extends to the map itself. The way in which information is brought to the viewer's attention may or may not relate to the order in which your map layers are stacked. The principal component of hierarchy within the map is called the **figure-to-ground organization**. The figure is defined as the object of attention, standing out from the background. The ground is the background space. In photography, this is sometimes achieved by blurring items in the background, drawing the eye to the figure with a crisp focus. In cartography, we have a number of tools to help us direct the viewer's attention.

Establishing strong figure-ground relationships is mainly about contrast. With mapping, this is often used to describe the contrast between land and water, but can also draw focus to specific parts of the land or ocean while diminishing the importance of other areas. We can alter values, textures, or colors, or add a bold outline to develop a strong edge. Line weights and symbols within the map can draw offerings to key information. Placement on the page and relationship to other elements also help us determine which parts of the map are the important parts as seen in the following figure:

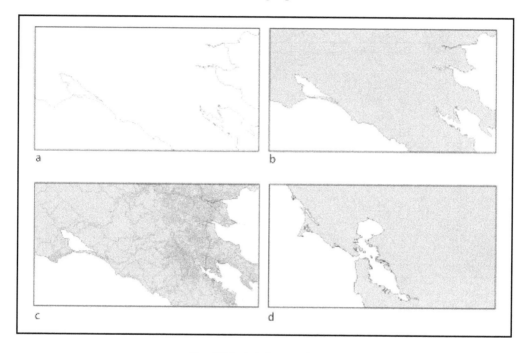

Figure 3.12: Developing figure-ground contrast

The previous figure demonstrates the development of figure-to-ground contrast. The previous, figure consists of four parts:

- **a**: There is no contrast, and the reader is unable to determine for certain what is happening in this picture.
- **b**: There is some effort to distinguish water from land, and if the reader is familiar with the shape of coastlines, they may be able to determine that the gray area is land, and the white is water.
- **c**: Further cements this certainty with the addition of roads.

- **d**: Establishes it through context, readers familiar with the area will recognize the shape of San Francisco Bay. It should be noted that in, *Figure 3.12(d)*, would be ineffective for readers unfamiliar with this shape, and other means would be necessary. The addition of labels, of course, would further improve distinction between land and water, and a strong coastal outline would help focus the eye.

In our **New Zealand** map, we can apply the same technique we used in earlier maps, and add a nice, thick coastline to make the land pop. We'll also add some other features to reinforce the impression:

1. Set the **Symbology** for the **NZ outline** to black and **3 pt** width.
2. Expand the **Map Frame** in the **Contents** pane and turn on the **Roads and Regions** layers in the **NZ** map.

While this map is less ambiguous than the San Francisco Bay example (*Figure 3.12*), we now have a clear delineation between land and water. This also makes the islands much heavier and helps retain focus in the center of the page, so it isn't overpowered by the bold title working to balance any potentially heavy legend items.

This hierarchy also applies between important and less important map features as well. We'll spend more time on how to achieve clean, uncluttered maps in `Chapter 8`, *Clean Symbology and Uncluttered Maps*; but for now, just be alert to the change in the balance of your map, as you direct the reader's focus through figure-ground contrast.

Creating unity

Unity is the interrelationship of map elements. It isn't about making everything identical, but rather complimentary. Neatlines don't have to all be the same thickness, but they should work together to support the balance and hierarchy of your elements. Fonts and colors should be limited and coordinated (more on this in later chapters). Patterns should vary in intensity, rather than style.

You see examples of unity every day, in corporate branding. You might be expected to produce maps with certain aspects already specified, such as your organization's logo or colors. You might also be part of a team that is producing a series of maps, and you need to make all of the maps look like they belong together. Sometimes this can pose challenges if these restrictions don't mix well with what's happening in your map, but there are ways to bring it all together.

Unity also refers to lining things up, making them look like they are part of a set—not in rigid conformity, but in a way that supports regular forms and doesn't interfere with balance. We saw this a little in, *Figure 3.4*, but in the following figure, it shows what can sometimes happen if default placement is used:

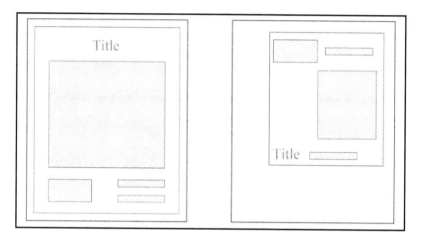

Figure 3.13: Left, a pleasing alignment of elements. Right, a jumble of elements that distracts the eye.

Let's revisit our **New Zealand** map, and make sure all the elements are working together. We'll do more with fonts in `Chapter 4`, *Typographic Principles*, but for now, let's make sure that the fonts in our legend, scale bar, and map credits all match:

1. Select the **Scale Bar** and set the **Numbers** and **Units** to **Arial**, **8 pt**.
2. Select the credits—name, date and source and set them to **Arial**, **8 pt**.
3. Set the title to **Arial Black**, **24 pt** or **36 pt**, depending on how you've balanced your other items.
4. Delete your legend placeholder. If you didn't turn on the **Roads and Regions** layers in the last section, do so now.
5. On the **Insert** tab, click **Legend**. Click and drag a box over the spot where your placeholder was.
6. Double-click on the **Legend** to launch the **Format** pane.
7. Switch to **Text Symbol** and expand **Appearance**. Set the font to **Arial**, **12 pt**.
8. In the **Contents** pane, expand the **Legend** to show each item. Uncheck **NZ Outline** and **NZ _Dissolve**, as these are unneeded.

Now that you've got an actual legend in, reassess your overall balance and see if anything needs to be adjusted. Remember that the compilation process is just a rough draft to help quickly position elements, not a final draft. Here's just one possibility:

Figure 3.14: Sample layout with unified map elements

Working with multiple data frames

Adding insets or small multiples can be as much about clarity as it is about leading your map reader through the map in a specific way. In Chapter 2, *Getting Started in ArcGIS Pro,* we have added a **Locator Map** to remind our map reader of the general location of our map data. For some maps, this is not necessary if the audience is likely to know where it is already (for example, a local map for a city council meeting), or it is such a clearly recognizable place (for example, the African continent). It's important to assess your target audience and decide if a locator adds value.

An inset map adds more detail about a specific area of the map. Insets are common on road maps, where the network of streets becomes too dense for clarity in urban centers, or to draw attention to a specific set of features on the map, as seen in the following figure. In this case, the inset is also floated over parts of the map to demonstrate its relative importance:

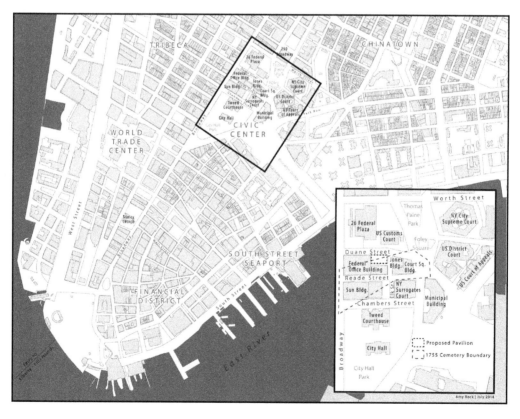

Figure 3.15: An inset map adds clarity and focus to specific areas of the map

Either of these can be created from new maps, or by adding a **Map Frame** into your layout a second time, and changing the extent, if all relevant data layers are present.

You can also insert data frames to create small multiples. A small multiple is a technique popularized by Edward Tufte for visualizing the change. As the name implies, they are multiple copies of the same map at the same small scale with little detail, to highlight changes in the data. They are a great technique for displaying the same variable at different time periods, or different variables over the same geographic extent. By repeating the same base layer at the same scale, the reader is focused on the change between maps rather than the marginalia.

Small multiples are rendered at the same scale, and organized in a line or grid to allow quick comparison. To see them in action, let's set up a new project and use our **US Counties** data:

1. Open a new project and select **Blank Project**
2. Insert a **New Map**
3. Right-click and remove the **Topographic** layer that automatically appears

When you add a new map to a project, ArcPro tries to save you time by including an Esri basemap. You can change this setting in **Project | Options**. Under **Map and Scene**, choose a **Default basemap of your organization,** or select **None** to create your own beautiful maps from scratch.

4. Add the **US Counties** layer from your GettingStarted folder
5. Click on the symbol for **UScounties** to open the **Symbology** pane
6. Change the method from **Single Symbol** to **Graduated Colors**
7. Set the **Field** to **VACANT** and **Normalization** to **HSE_UNITS**, to display the percentage of housing units that are vacant
8. Leave the method on **Natural Breaks** and set the **Classes** to **5**
9. Click the drop-down for **Color scheme**, and check the box next to **Show names**
10. Select reds (5 classes)
11. Click the **More** button over the classifications, and select **Symbols | Format all symbols**
12. Set the **Outline color** to Soapstone Dust and the **Width** to **0.4 pt**

13. Click **Apply** and the back arrow (at the top of the pane) to return to the classification scheme

14. Click anywhere to deselect the classes, then click the lightest symbol

15. Change the **Outline color** to Sahara Sand and click **Apply** (this helps reduce the amount of detail when the map size is reduced)

 When displaying maps at a very small scale, often the symbol outlines can overwhelm the symbol color. Turning off outlines often results in an undesirable loss of detail. For best effect, set the **Outline color** slightly darker than the symbol color, and the outline as thin as possible.

Add three more map frames, and choose some variables from the table. Since this is just for practice, they don't need to necessarily make sense together. Don't forget to normalize where appropriate:

1. Insert a **New Layout**. Select **ANSI Letter**, **Landscape** orientation.

2. Add in print margin guides.

3. Insert each of your **Map Frame**—use the selection next to the **Default** to have them insert at a less than full page.

4. Select each **Map Frame** in turn, and on the **Format** tab, set the **Width** to **5** inches and height to **3.25** inches.

5. Align the bottom two frames with the margin guides in the corners.

6. Align the top two frames with the side margin guides.

7. Select each frame in turn, and set the **Scale** (in the lower-left corner of the layout window) to **1:40,000,000**. You may need to type it in for the first one, and then it will be available in the list for the rest of them.

8. Select all four map frames (hold the *Shift* key and click each one) and on the **Format** tab, change the **Current Selection** to **Border**, and set the **Line** to **No Color**.

9. To complete your small multiples, you may need to add in legends, but keep them small and unobtrusive, the maps should tell the story.

10. Add a title that encapsulates the series, feel free to have a little fun since we're just playing with the data.

Remember, once you have a **Map Frame** or map element positioned and formatted just the way you want, you can lock it to keep from accidentally moving or changing it. Just click the padlock next to the item in the **Contents** pane.

Here's a completely random data series presented as small multiples:

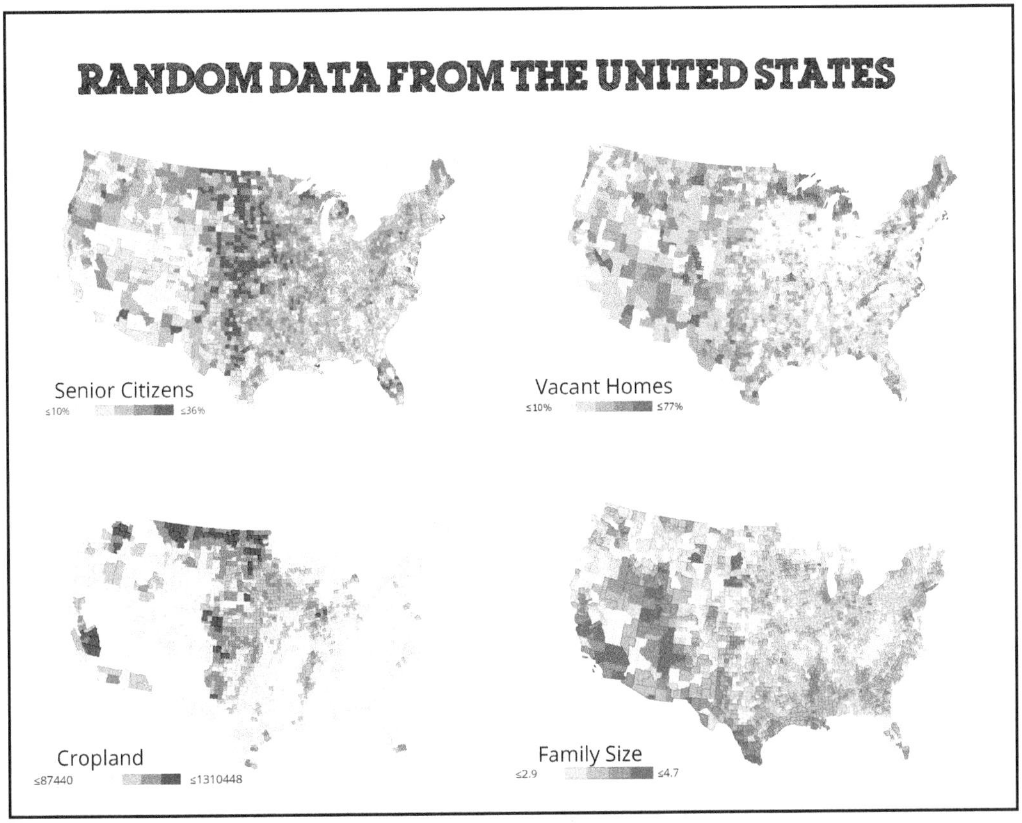

Figure 3.16: Small multiples sample

Planning out your map

The most important thing when putting together a map is to plan it out with a compilation sketch, whether it's digital, or old-school paper and pencil. Too often, we rush through to meet a deadline and end up with a poorly planned map that doesn't get its message across clearly. Even though it is much simpler in ArcPro to add, move, and reuse maps and layouts, planning is still essential.

At a minimum, toss some placeholder rectangles in your layout view as you work. This is especially important if you know you will have a sizeable legend, inset, or locator maps, or if you need to add charts or notes to the map. If you don't plan for them early, you may wind up wasting precious time moving and resizing things to make it all fit, and run out of either time or patience to focus on those three themes of balance, harmony, and unity that will make your map shine. When everything is in place, lean back and give it the squint test—close your eyes halfway, and see if something jumps out that shouldn't, or vice versa.

One last thing, sometimes you can leave out certain map elements. Certainly, if you're working with small multiples, you make all the maps at the same scale, so you only need one set of scale and directional indicators. If you've used a graticule, you don't need a north arrow. If everything on your map is labeled, you don't need a legend. Is the map going in a report, or professional publication? You might be able to put the title in the caption and free up some space, although if it's likely the map will be shared independently of the report, you may want to leave it in. Don't just automatically stuff everything in there; make sure it makes sense.

Practice on your own

Take any of the sample layouts in this project, and prepare a compilation sheet for an inset or locator map, or set up small multiples with three or more map frames.

Summary

In this chapter, we investigated the three key elements of good cartographic design—balance, harmony, and unity. Balance is key to keeping the reader's attention focused on the center of the page. Harmony helps the important parts of our map message shine through. Unity ties it all together with a professional, well-composed presentation. We looked at these concepts as applied to all elements that make up a map layout, then rounded out our discussion of multiple map frames with an introduction to small multiples, one of the most effective data visualization techniques for presenting volumes of data in a small space.

In the next chapter, we'll look at typography in maps, from selecting font pairings to placement and map grammar. We'll also learn some tools for labeling efficiency by creating reusable styles, and setting preferences for dynamic labeling.

4
Typographic Principles

Text on maps should never be done casually, but with the deliberate planning of both placement and design. From the eye-catching title blocks of Sanborn Fire Maps and the distinctive fonts of National Geographic to the clean hierarchy of Swiss topographical maps, the role of typography in maps is an important one that can enhance or undermine the value of a map. In this chapter, we will look at the form and function of text on maps, from a brief discussion of the psychology of type and the anatomy of letterforms, to pairing fonts and building map grammar through consistent styling. Finally, we'll walk through translating those design choices into label styles and work with the **Maplex Label Engine** to quickly and consistently apply labels to our maps.

In this chapter, we will cover the following topics:

- Using type on maps
- Understanding letterforms
- Choosing and pairing fonts
- Building map grammar
- Labeling in ArcGIS Pro

Using type on maps

Map titles are an excellent place to set the mood of the map, and then carry it through with labeling and color choices. The ornate title blocks, or cartouches, of the Sanborn Map Company, were an important part of their branding. The maps themselves conveyed the accuracy and reliability of the data with crisp linework and draftsman's labeling. By contrast, the cartouches were highly elaborate, calling to mind detailed copper engravings and official documents, creating a recognizable product.

Perhaps a more ubiquitous example of typography and mood on maps can be found between the pages of National Geographic magazine. These detailed maps are often accompanied by blocks of text or rich illustrations, and are easily recognizable as National Geographic products even before you spot that **Telltale** yellow rectangle. There's a reason for this—their team of cartographers works from a detailed, pages-long style manual that specifies font styles for every type and size of feature. Labeling countries in a region? There's a style for that. Cultural regions? Bodies of water? Wildlife habitat? Disputed areas? You guessed it—there's a style for them all. The fonts, carefully selected and periodically evaluated, are designed to convey a scientific gravitas, but with a little flair that makes it distinctive.

While National Geographic may use some of the most familiar label styling, many other organizations also have consistent, branded style guides. Many public and private map companies have distinct styles that provide clarity but also set a mood, and perhaps even clearly identify the publisher. Independent cartographers often have more freedom to exercise their creativity, but regardless of personal preference, the intended audience for the map must ultimately dictate the mood. Road maps done in a swashbuckling script might look fun, but be frustratingly illegible when you are lost, or seem less reliable than a more traditional font. Whole books have been written on the use (and misuse) of typography, and provide insight into the way we respond to typefaces.

But aside from all of this branding and subtle psychological impact, the ultimate goal of lettering on maps is to enhance communication. Eduard Imhof, the renowned Swiss cartographer, made the most of the interplay between science and art in cartography, and in his paper, *Positioning Names on Maps* (Eduard Imhof, 1975), provided a number of guidelines for label placement and label form that are still widely regarded as canon by cartographers today. These guidelines were set forth not as Imhof's personal aesthetic, but rather as an attempt to document the collective knowledge of cartographers, which is perhaps why this document is still so salient. His key principles tie directly to map communication—legibility, clear connection between names and features, hierarchy, and the selection of features to label. We'll look at his specific guidance for points, lines, and areas in more detail as we generate label styles in ArcGIS Pro.

Understanding letterforms

As mapmakers, we may be tempted to simply jump in and choose a font that looks right for our map, but an understanding of some key elements of letterforms can help define why a particular font works with the rest of our map elements or not. While there are many components to letterforms, for our purposes, we only need to concentrate on a few, shown in the following figure:

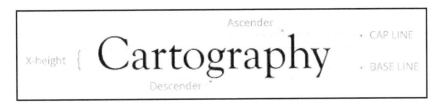

Figure 4.1: Anatomy of letterforms

Picture a sheet of notebook paper. The light blue lines printed on it correspond to the **BASE LINE** and the **CAP LINE** in the preceding figure. **Ascender** and **Descender** often extend over and under these lines, which can sometimes conflict with other map features (if too extensive), and can impact legibility in blocks of text. The **X-height** is the height of the body of a lowercase letter, which, in part, helps determine the visual weight of a font. If the x-height and the cap line are fairly close together, the font will appear heavier and more compact than if they are farther apart.

Leading, tracking, and kerning help determine the amount of white space in a label or paragraph. **Leading** refers to the space between base lines, which, in manual typesetting, was created by placing a thin strip of lead between the rows of type blocks. In ArcGIS Pro, leading is set using the **Line spacing** options under **Text Symbol** in the **Format Text**:

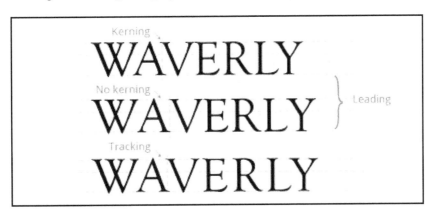

Figure 4.2: Leading, tracking, and kerning

Kerning and tracking refer to the spaces between individual letters, but each has a specific function. **Tracking** allows you to spread letters out (which is helpful for labeling area features), or to compress them slightly to fit into tight spaces, and is controlled using the **Letter spacing** settings. Too much expansion or compression can impair readability, so this setting should be changed with care.

Kerning adjusts the spacing between letters to nest them slightly, so that gaps between narrower letters don't appear larger than those between wide ones, as shown in, *Figure 4.2*. Kerning is turned on by default in ArcGIS Pro, but if you want to disable it for some reason, just turn off the checkbox. Be aware that turning off kerning may not be an obvious difference in some fonts, but can greatly impact legibility in areas of dense labeling.

One last factor that impacts the way labels look on the map is the choice between serif and sans-serif. Serifs are the little flourishes that stick out at the edges of letters, and can impact visual weight, mood, and legibility and play a key role in the development of map grammar, detailed later in this chapter. Serifs can come in a variety of styles, which can increase or decrease the visual weight and change the flavor of the map, as shown in the following figure:

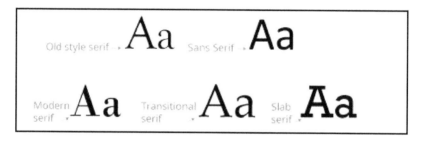

Figure 4.3: Serif and sans-serif styles

A general rule for lettering on maps is to never go smaller than 6 point type, but the size of the type may not appear to be consistent between fonts. Font size is based on points, which refer to the size of the block on which movable type was set. A one inch block holds 72 point font, but because of block positioning (accommodating ascenders and descenders) and the comparative roundness of letters, not all fonts appear the same at the same size, as seen in the following figure:

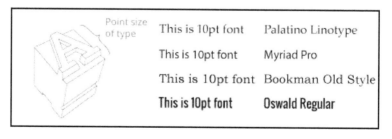

Figure 4.4: Sizing type

Choosing and pairing fonts

Fonts do more than just dress up our labels. Researchers have found significant connections between typeface choice and whether or not readers find the information to be credible. Certain fonts, such as Baskerville and Computer Modern, are often considered to be authoritative fonts, often used in scholarly publications because of their ability to disappear, leaving the reader focused on the information and not the font. *Helvetica*, outlined in the film of the same name, gained credibility in the business world as a solid, no-nonsense response to the often whimsical logos and advertisements of the 1950s. Its clean, solid lines let readers know the product is solid and trustworthy.

It's important to pay attention to the subconscious clues provided by the map's text in relation to the map's purpose. A map about a significant health threat, for example, should never be done in Comic Sans. While many cartographers will tell you there's never a good reason to use Comic Sans, its name certainly gives a clue to the sort of mood it will imply on your map. Serious maps require serious fonts, but that doesn't always mean old-fashioned or boring. Sometimes our maps can explore the whimsical side, such as maps for tourism or younger audiences. In those cases, a reliable, scholarly font might very well ruin the mood. It's also important to avoid cliché fonts, such as maps of Egypt done in Papyrus, or maps of Greece labeled in Lithos.

Choosing fonts

Choosing fonts should be about four primary things—legibility, readability, mood, and hierarchy. Legibility is paramount; no matter how fun that retro script font looks, if no one can read the labels, your map is useless, so use ornate fonts sparingly. Legibility also extends to individual letters—lowercase *i*, *l*, and *j* (as well as capital *I* and lowercase *l*) should be distinct, as should *c* and *e*. In a paragraph of text, these letters can often be assumed by context, but when used in isolated labels, particularly if the reader is unfamiliar with the subject area, context is not always present.

Legibility is by and large about the shape of the letters themselves. As we learn to read, we develop the ability to recognize the silhouettes of letters, thereby speeding our ability to read whole words. Labels in proper case (first letter capitalized and all others in lowercase) are read more quickly than labels in all caps. Our eyes have to slow down and look more closely at the blockier capital letters, which can be an important way to emphasize certain labels, but exhausting to the reader if overused. For this same reason, many consider serif fonts easier to read, because the shapes of letters are more distinct, but if your labeling is not overly dense, sans-serif may be equally legible.

Readability is more about the amount of whitespace in and around your labels. While this is often an issue more relevant for paragraphs of text, it can also apply to areas of dense labeling. A dense, heavy font means you will need to leave more space around each label to keep it readable, so if you've got a lot of labels to fit into an area, choose something lighter. And, if you do have blocks of text elsewhere on your map spread, you'll want those to coordinate with your map, so plan ahead.

Mood relates directly to the underlying psychology of fonts; there are some quick guidelines that can help us capture the right feel for our map. Typefaces with old style or transitional serifs convey dignity and a sense of tradition. Bold, slab serifs, and even modern serifs with considerable differences between the thick and thin strokes, convey power and strength. Sans-serif is often associated with precision, with the exception of some more frivolous fonts like the aforementioned Papyrus, Lithos, or Comic Sans. Fonts with irregular x-heights (for example, smaller vowels) can generate a certain amount of visual energy and excitement, but be careful not to compete with your actual map data. Scripts and italic forms of some of the old style fonts can imply elegance (think wedding invitations), but for mapmakers, they are typically used for water labels. It's often best to confine these to large bodies of water; a fancy script Pacific Ocean is going to be far more legible than a river in the same font.

In Chapter 3, *Organizing the Page Structure,* we discussed building an overall map hierarchy to lead your reader through the information in a logical way and help them prioritize important elements. Labels are an absolutely critical part of map hierarchy, and, because of their natural tendency to float to the top of the viewer's attention, can make or break the hierarchy of the entire map. Larger cities should have bolder and larger labels than smaller cities, although too much boldness can impair legibility, so use caution. In general, area labels should be softer, as their typically larger extent lends them more weight than usual. Important features should stand out from less important or contextual items. This can be done through the size and weight of an individual font, or through the use of an additional font.

This brings us to a discussion of what to do when labeling everything on the map in the same font isn't feasible; perhaps you have several sizes of cities, some landmarks, and a whole taxonomy of natural features, all in the same map. Compatibility of fonts is as important as the choice of fonts themselves. Font pairing, like wine and cheese, relies on contrast, but conflict can be jarring to the palette.

Pairing fonts

A quick and easy font pairing starts with selecting one serif and one sans-serif font. We know that serif fonts are often easier for people to read, so they make a great body font for maps with paragraph text, and are often used for natural features on maps. Most have a lovely italic font that makes great water feature labels, and their serifs remind us that nature is often not easily confined to straight lines. For that reason, Baskerville and Garamond and Source Serif Pro, and a number of other great fonts for books and blogs, also work well for map labels.

To get the most out of this pairing, look for sans-serif fonts with similar shapes and visual feels. Try to keep other elements similar. Are the Os rounded or oval? Are the x-heights similar? In this case, the contrast between serif and sans-serif will generally provide all the variation you need, without adding a lot of distraction.

Pairing two sans-serif fonts can be more challenging. Some guidelines include matching a bold font with a light one (which can sometimes be done within the same font family), or a rounded one with a condensed, oval form. Since your contrast needs to be done entirely without the aid of serifs, you'll need to have clear distinctions and roles for each font. Sometimes, type foundries will design a group of fonts specifically to work together, which makes your life easier. Look for who designed the type when browsing font sites, and see if they have made others. There are also numerous font pairing sites that will do the hard work for you, leaving you to select the overall visual impression you like from a selection of well-matched fonts.

Finally, when choosing a font, be sure to explore all of its characters and glyphs to make sure you have what you need. This is especially critical if you are labeling in a language that uses diacritics, which are not always included. And pay careful attention to numbers if you'll be using them in your map. Some fonts that are clean and gorgeous in the letter department have scrunched, hard to read numbers. If you've already downloaded the font, you can launch the **Character Map** in Windows (**Start**|**Search**|**Character Map**) and scroll through the entire character set.

Of course, you can bypass the whole pairings process and select a font family with lots of options. Font families are a single font, with all of its variations in form, width, and weight. Form refers to roman (regular or upright) and italic (slanted) type, upper and lowercase, and also whether or not a font has a true small caps option. Width refers to the width of individual letters, and falls into three categories—regular, condensed, and expanded or extended, and sometimes additional levels of condensed or expanded.

Weight generally ranges from light or thin to extrabold or black, with one or more levels in between. Some families have more options than others. In the following figure, **Open Sans** is displayed in a variety of weights and widths, in regular and italic forms. While not all combinations are available, there are enough variations to develop significant hierarchy without ever changing fonts:

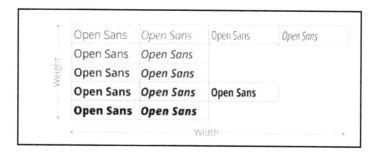

Figure 4.5: Open Sans font family

While you probably already have quite an assortment of fonts on your computer, you can always add more. There are a number of font sources available on the internet, including Dafont (www.dafont.com) and Font Squirrel (www.fontsquirrel.com). Font Squirrel also has a Matcherator, which allows you to upload an image and identify the font used in it. These sites, and many others, have a variety of fonts with a variety of licensing options, and most have a preview option where you can test out your most challenging labels. Many are free to download, but be sure to check the use restrictions; some are not available for commercial use, some require a small fee to use commercially, and others are completely free to use for personal or commercial applications. It's also important to make sure you get a **TrueType** (**TT**) or **OpenType** (**OT**) font, as fonts without this designation may not render clearly in your final map.

One final caveat as you dive down the rabbit hole of font selection—obey the three font rule. Maps should never have more than three distinct fonts, and preferably only two, plus a fancy title. More than that, and your map reader is going to feel overwhelmed.

Building map grammar

When we develop a system of font styles, we are essentially building the grammar of the map. The combination of labels and symbols helps our audience learn new features by comparing them to the structures used for familiar features.

The first piece of this is the map hierarchy. When we assign fonts by feature class, size, or importance, we are helping our map reader quickly determine which parts of the map should be viewed first. Large, bold fonts leap forward and demand attention, while smaller and lighter fonts recede, providing information when needed, but not assertively.

We can also use fonts as variables. The contrast between serif and sans-serif lends itself to qualitative distinctions. Any time we change fonts, even if they are both serif or sans-serif, we are clueing our reader into a change in information. Color, form, and width can also indicate qualitative changes, but be careful they don't move to a different place in the hierarchy by appearing heavier or lighter.

Quantitative changes are perhaps easier to indicate through size and weight, and also the use of uppercase. Color can sometimes indicate quantitative change, if using lighter and darker values of a single hue, for example.

The determination of what is important on a map can merely be a factor of size, but may also be linked to the purpose of the map. A city central to the topic may be represented in a heavier font than a larger city appearing on the map. Remember that the point of map grammar is to lead your user through the information in a coherent way.

Regardless of which features carry more weight and why, it is absolutely important to not overpower the map with labels, and that legibility is not impaired.

Labeling in ArcGIS Pro

A great deal of labeling in ArcGIS Pro can be handled dynamically, by customizing settings in the **Maplex Label Engine**. We'll look at the options, then add a few custom touches at the end. Before you begin labeling, you may want to outline a rough style sheet for your features. In this walk-through, we'll be using Open Sans and Baskerville, which can be downloaded from Font Squirrel (`www.fontsquirrel.com`). You may also substitute fonts of your choice. The following are the steps involved:

1. Open the sample typography project, `MNTypography.aprx`. Take a moment to explore the project, which has point, line, and area features pared down for the purposes of our practice.
2. Notice that **St. Paul** (the capital) is in a separate layer from the rest of the cities. This allows more flexibility of symbolization, which we'll discuss later, in `Chapter 8`, *Clean Symbology and Uncluttered Maps*.

3. Before we go any further, let's verify that the **Maplex Label Engine** is turned on. Maplex offers greater customization than the standard label engine, which means less manual cleanup work after adding labels. In ArcGIS Pro, this should be turned on by default, but you can verify this on the **Map** tab. In the **Labeling** section, click **More,** and make sure **Use Maplex Label Engine** is checked.

4. Features to be labeled in this map are as follows—cities, highways, rivers, lakes, and counties. A sample style sheet is outlined in the following table. You don't need to decide all at once, but it's helpful to have a rough plan and update as you go. The following table helps in labeling the style sheet:

Feature	Label style
St. Paul	Open Sans, Extrabold, 14 pt, all caps, 10% gray halo.
Small cities	Open Sans, Regular, 10 pt, 10% gray halo.
Medium cities	Open Sans, Semibold, 12 pt, 10% gray halo.
Large cities (Minneapolis)	Open Sans, Extrabold, 14 pt, regular case, 10% gray halo.
Interstates	BW Interstate shield, Open Sans, Semibold, 7 pt.
US Highways	US Highway shield, Open Sans, Semibold, 7 pt.
Rivers	Open Sans, Light Italic, 10 pt.
Lakes	Open Sans, Light Italic, 10 pt-12 pt.
Counties	Open Sans, Light, 8 pt, all caps.

Working with point features

When labeling point features, it is important to place the label in a position that makes it clear which point it belongs to, especially in areas of dense labels. The following figure shows the preferred order of placement for point features, with an example of each. The preferred placement is right and slightly over (position **1**), so that the baseline of the text is aligned with the top of the point feature. Right and slightly under (position **2**) is also easily interpreted by the reader. Continue through the positions in order, but if it comes to placement in position **7** or position **8**, you may want to see if you can move other labels to make room. As you can see in the example, 7 and 8 can lead to clarity issues, depending on the font and symbol used.

Callouts and lines should never be used, except in extreme circumstances; rearrange other labels or reduce the number of point features, if possible. An inset map may be the best choice for dense areas:

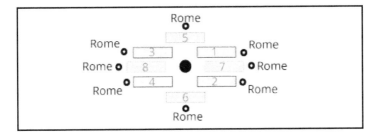

Figure 4.6: Positioning point labels

There should never be space between letters in a point feature label, and the use of expanded fonts can also be misleading. Labels should be horizontal unless you are aligning to the graticule, in which case a gentle curve to match the latitude lines is best. It is also important to keep the label snug enough to the point so it clearly identifies it, but without crowding, as seen in the following figure:

Figure 4.7: Placement relative to point feature

Point feature labels should never be split between land and water (that is, falling off a coastline), and, where possible, should be labeled on the side of the river where the majority of the feature lies. If the shape of the coastline or river prohibits clean horizontal placement, you may need to be creative. In these cases, it is often helpful to reference other maps of the area and see how they handled the situation, then base your solution on the one that is the easiest to read and interpret. Labels should never overlap, and should never appear to be lying on their back, or upside down, from the map reader's viewpoint. Let's practice these:

1. Return to the **Twin Cities** bookmark (**Bookmarks|Twin Cities**).
2. Right-click on **St_Paul** in the **Contents** pane and select **Label**. This will automatically label **St. Paul**.

3. Right-click again and select **Labeling Properties**. In the **Label Class** pane, click on **Position**. The placement defaults to best position, which is determined by the **Zones** wheel underneath. Reset the numbers as shown, to match Imhof's guidelines in, *Figure 4.6*. When complete, your **Zones** wheel should look like the following figure:

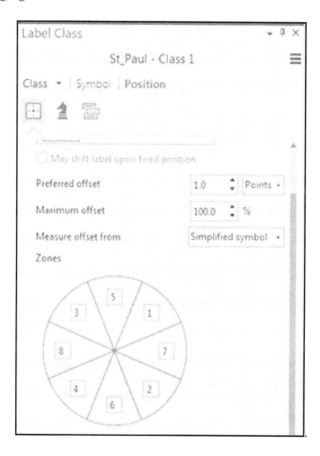

Figure 4.8: Customizing placement zones

4. Since we don't want to recreate this **Zones** wheel every time we label point features, let's save it to a style. Click on the **Menu** button (≡) and select **Save position to style**. Name it `Imhof points`, and add a **Category** and **Tags** to help you find it again later, as shown in the following figure:

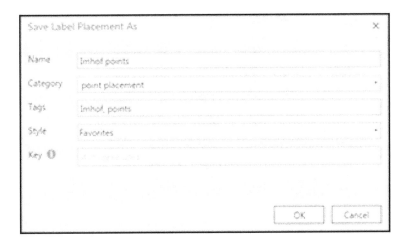

Figure 4.9: Saving placement settings to a style

5. Switch to the **Symbol** tab to set the appearance. Since **St. Paul** is the capital, and also one of the largest cities, we want to make it reasonably large and heavy in the hierarchy.

6. In the **General** settings, expand **Appearance** and set the **Font name** to **Open Sans** (or your equivalent choice), **Font style** to **Extrabold,** and size to **14 pt**.

7. Set the **Text case** to **Upper case**.

8. **St. Paul** crosses several lines, so to improve readability, let's add a subtle halo to block out the lines behind the letters. Scroll down to **Halo** and expand it.

9. Set the **Halo symbol** to white fill, and the **Color** to gray 10%. You can ignore **Outline color** and leave the **Outline width** at **0 pt**.

 Masking (adding an outline or halo to your text) will magnify the effects of serifs and decorative fonts, and generally adds noise to the map, so it should be done subtly, and only when necessary.

10. Set the **Halo size** to **1.5 pt**. This is a little large, but we want **St. Paul** to be really clear.

11. Click **Apply**. Notice how the label now appears to interrupt the line slightly, as shown in the following figure, but there is no distinct outline to the letters (obviously, we're already bending some rules, and we're just getting started):

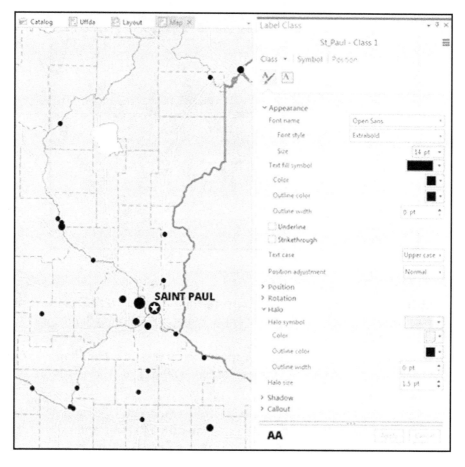

Figure 4.10: Setting symbol properties for the St. Paul label

12. The rest of the cities are in a single layer, classified by population. Right-click on **MNCities** in the **Contents** pane and select **Label**.

Did you notice how the **St. Paul** label shifted? That's ArcGIS Pro's dynamic labeling at work. As you add labels to the map, other labels will shift around to accommodate each set of rules as best it can.

13. For this layer, we want to match the label styles to the symbol sizes, to reinforce the relative size of the cities. Right-click again and select **Labeling Properties**. In the **Label Class** pane, select **Class**.

14. By default, ArcGIS Pro starts you off with **Class 1**. Click on the **Menu** button (≡) in the top-right of the pane and select **Rename Label Class**.

15. Rename this class to <50K.

16. Click the **SQL** button to build your class in SQL, then click **Add Clause**.

17. We'll use the same clause as the symbology: **POP2007 is Less Than or Equal to 50000**. Click **Add**, then click **Apply**.

18. Set the symbol according to your style sheet, **Open Sans**, **Regular**, **10 pt**, 10% gray halo. Leave this halo at **1 pt** and click **Apply**.
    St. Paul has moved again and the rest of the city labels disappeared. Let's build two more label classes to bring them back. We're also going to save this style to make setting up the rest of the classes a breeze.

19. Click on the **Menu** button again and select **Save Symbol to Style**, like we did with our placement properties. Give your style a name, such as MNCities, and add a **Category** and **Tags** to help you find it again later.

20. Click on **Class** again, and then on the **Menu** button, and select **Create Label Class**. Let's call this one 50-100K. All the cities will appear again in the map (including the ones we already labeled), since we haven't defined which cities are in this label class.

21. Use the **SQL** button again to set the class to match the symbology. This one's a little more complicated, as we'll need two clauses: **POP2007 is Greater Than 50000** and **POP2007 is Less Than or Equal to 100000**.

22. Click **Apply,** and the extra labels should disappear.

23. Since we saved the last class as a style, we can apply and modify it to save time formatting this class. On the **Feature Layer** context ribbon, select the **Labeling** tab.

24. In the **Text Symbol** section, you should see your **MNcities** style. (If you don't see it, click the drop-down menu and select **More**, then search for it using your **Category** or **Tags**.) Select it to **Apply** it to this **Class**.

25. We want the medium cities to stand out from the small cities, so in that same part of the ribbon, set the **Font size** to **12** and the **Font style** to **Semibold**.

26. Repeat the process to create the 100+ class (which contains only Minneapolis), with the **SQL** clause set to **POP2007 is Greater Than 100000**, and the **MNCities** style customized to **14 pt** and **Extrabold**.
   You may notice some things that you don't like happening with the labels. That's because we didn't set the placement properties when we created these label classes.

27. On the ribbon, set the **Class** (far left) to **<50k** and at the far right, set the **Label Placement** to **Imhof points**. This will clean up most of the conflicts.

28. Since there's a nice clear area to the lower-right of **St. Paul**, we can go back to the **Placement** settings for that layer and set the placement to **Bottom right of point**. This clears up almost all the conflicts, except for Minneapolis, which is overlapping the symbol for **St. Paul**.

29. Switch to the **MNCities** layer and the 100+ class, and set the position to **Bottom left of point**.

By setting specific placements for the two large cities, the rest of the cities can use the rules we set to dynamically fit themselves around these two features and save us a lot of manual adjustment.

Working with line features

Line features can be some of the most difficult features to label. Linear features should always follow the line, and be labeled above the line, almost as if the feature were underlining the label, but with a tiny bit of space underneath, as seen in the *Figure 4.11*. Look for the smoothest stretch near where you want to place the label, and generally horizontal, if you can manage it. It is still not appropriate to put spaces between letters, but you can put spaces between words on long stretches. Be careful not to add so much space that the reader has already forgotten the first part by the time they reach the second:

Figure 4.11: Labeling along a line

A widely used cartographic convention is to label water features in italics. The slight sense of motion that italics implies corresponds well to the fluidity of water. This can sometimes create some interesting issues when splining text along a line. A quick workaround can be to insert a space between two problem letters or shift the whole label by adding space at the beginning or between words.

When line features are represented as a polygon, such as with wide rivers, text may be centered inside the feature (that is, in the river), but following the remaining placement guidelines for linear features. As with point features, labels should never appear upside down to the map reader. Let's work on some line features:

1. Right-click on **MajorMNRivers** in the **Contents** pane and select **Label**. Notice that some rivers are labeled in multiple places.

2. Right-click again and select **Labeling Properties**. In the **Label Class** pane, select **Position**, and then click the **Conflict Resolution** icon.

3. Expand **Remove duplicate** labels and select **Remove All**. This will leave you with one label per river, which is plenty at this scale. For smaller scale maps, you can use **Remove within fixed distance** to set a preferred distance between labels.

4. Click the **Position** icon, expand **Placement,** and select **River Placement**. This will spline the text along the river.

5. If some of the labels appear upside down, expand **Orientation** and make sure **Align label to direction of line** is not checked. While this can be useful for some specific applications, it can result in some labels appearing upside down. Avoid using this setting unless your particular use case requires labeling along feature direction.

6. Lastly, we'll change the symbol to match our style sheet, **Open Sans**, **Light Italic**, **10 pt**. Click **Apply**, and notice that some city labels may move to accommodate the river labels.

7. Save this to a style, as we'll use it again for our lakes.

Once you make changes to your text symbol, you may notice some labels extend past the end of the line. To prevent this, click the **Fitting Strategy** icon, expand **Overrun,** and set it to **0 pt**.

An exception to the splining rule for linear features is when you are labeling them with icons, such as highway shields. The **MajorMNRoads** layer contains interstates and US highways, so we'll label them each with their respective shields:

1. Right-click on **MajorMNRoads** in the **Contents** pane and select **Label**. Notice that the labels say only **I** or **U**, and, like the rivers, are repeated.

2. Right-click again and select **Labeling Properties**. We want to label interstates and US highways separately, so let's create a label class for interstates. Start by renaming **Class 1** to `Interstates`.

3. Set the **SQL** clause to **HWY_TYPE is Equal to I**, and click **Apply**.

4. We need to get rid of the **I** and label the roads with their number, so in the **Feature Layer** context ribbon, on the **Labeling** tab, set the **Field** to **HWY_SYMBOL**.

5. In the **Text Symbol** section, select **Shield 1** as the symbol style. This will convert all the road numbers to road numbers on an interstate shield.

6. Highway shields should always be horizontal, so in the **Label Placement** section of the ribbon, select **Shield**.

7. Clear out duplicate labels like we did with the rivers. In the **Label Class** pane, select **Position**, and then click the **Conflict Resolution** icon.

8. Expand **Remove duplicate labels** and select **Remove All**. Again, if you need periodic labels along the length, you can use **Remove within fixed distance** to set a preferred distance between labels.

Since we're building this map in black and white, we'll need a grayscale version of the shield. This can be a little tricky to build in ArcGIS Pro, but you can work around this by using a point file. For this exercise, we'll make one by copying our `St. Paul` file:

1. Right-click on the **St. Paul** layer and click **Copy**.

2. Right-click on the **Map Frame** in the **Contents** pane and click **Paste**. This will put a second St. Paul layer in your map.

3. Rename it to **ShieldCustomization** and set the **Point Symbol** to the **Shield 1** symbol in the **Gallery**. A point will appear to the east of the **Twin Cities**.

4. Switch to the **Properties** tab, click the **Layers** icon, and notice that there are two components to this symbol—a red crest and a blue shield base.

5. Select the red crest and set the **Color** to Black.

6. Select the blue shield and set the **Color** to White.

7. Click **Apply**, then click the **Menu** button to save it to a style.

8. Turn the **ShieldCustomization** layer off. You may remove it from the map if you wish.

9. Return to the **Labeling properties** for **MajorMNRoads** and set the **Point Symbol** under **Callout** to your new symbol.

10. Repeat the process for the US highways, creating a label class, setting the **SQL** clause to **HWY_TYPE is Equal to U**, and using *Shield 7*.

Notice that the highway symbols are crowding out the city labels. Since this isn't intended to be a highway map, you can remove some of the offending labels by increasing the minimum feature size (under **Conflict Resolution**) until you are satisfied.

Working with area features

Area features should be labeled inside the feature, with regard to geometric extent, and may have space between letters so they stretch across a feature. They don't need to stretch across the entire extent in most cases, but should be given enough space to indicate the vastness of the area they represent. Try to balance the label in the space, allowing for other features and labels which may need to coexist inside the feature. If the area feature is small, such as a small lake or political boundary, point labeling strategies should be used, even if other features in the same layer or class are labeled inside.

Again, labels should never appear upside down and should be placed horizontally where possible. If labels are not placed horizontally, they should deviate enough so that they don't just look like they're crooked:

1. Right-click on **Minnesota_Counties** in the **Contents** pane and select **Label**. Notice that the labels say only **I** or **U**, and, like the rivers, are repeated.
2. Right-click again and select **Labeling Properties**.
3. Set the font as defined in our classes (**Open Sans**, **Light**, **8 pt**, **Upper case**), and set the **Placement** to **Land Parcel Placement**. You may also wish to set the **Font color** to gray 70%, to push it a little farther into the background and improve hierarchy.
4. To spread the labels a bit across the extent, click the **Position** icon and expand **Spread labels**. Set it to **Spread letters up to a fixed limit** (spreading to fill feature can lead to some pretty ridiculous labels where short labels and large areas meet). The maximum value here is based on character width, so 100% means no more than one full letter's space between letters. Notice that the spacing changes depending on the size of the feature, which matches best practices.

Your map should look something like this:

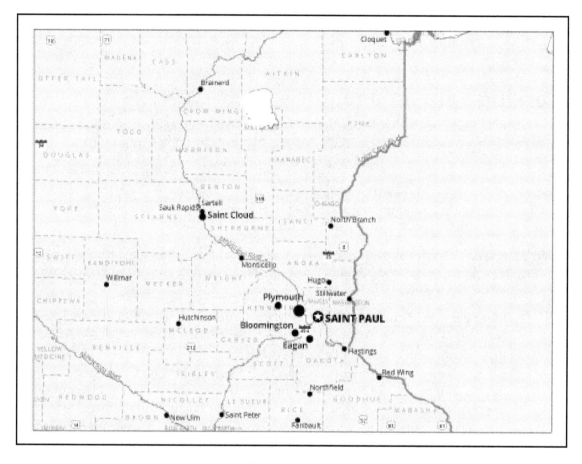

Figure 4.12: Sample results

Linear areas with no distinct lines, such as a mountain ridge, should be treated as a mix between line and area features. Letters can be spread along the feature, but since they will be built on a spline, it's important to maintain a constant arc, so it's evident the letters belong together.

Titles and other map elements

Titles should be the largest text on the map. Start between one and a half and two times the size of the largest feature label, and modify for balance. Use the **Text** tool on the **Insert** ribbon to add a text box, then format accordingly. In our example map, the largest labels are 14 pt, so your title should be at least 21 pt. Don't be afraid to go larger; the title is an important part of what draws in your audience. Titles can also overlap less important elements, like neighboring areas that provide context but aren't significant to the map message.

Legend elements should be in the same range as the majority of map labels. Most of our labels are in the 10-12pt range, so legend categories should be in that range, as well. The legend title can be slightly larger (say 14 pt), as long as that doesn't make it larger than any map labels.

Scale bars should be discreet; therefore, their labels should be quite small. These labels, and your source and other credits, should be the smallest text on the map, but don't drop beneath 6 pt, or it will become unreadable.

Practice on your own

Add labels to the lake features. Remember that small lakes can be labeled using point strategies, so you may want to set label classes based on size.

Summary

The key role of text on maps is to help communicate information more clearly. Labels should enhance the overall message and contribute to the visual hierarchy. Labels should never overwhelm the reader, either in quantity or in format. Remember that size equates to relative importance, so large, bold fonts should be used with caution. Capital letters also help to imply size and importance, and can be used quite effectively for large areas, but should be rationed elsewhere.

Fonts should be chosen with the map's audience in mind, so that the tone of the map is appropriate to the subject. Combining fonts should be done with care, and the total number of fonts should be minimized. Remember that many fonts have extensive font families that allow many distinct types of labels to be styled without adding noise.

In the next chapter, we'll look at the use of color in maps, and how that combines with the design and labeling principles we've already learned to enhance communication and mood. For further information you may refer to, Eduard Imhof, *Positioning Names on Maps: The American Cartographer, Vol. 2, No. 2,* October 1975.

5
Picking Colors with Confidence

Adding colors to maps is easy, but it's important to add them for the right reasons. When color is used appropriately on a map, the organization of the perceptual dimensions of color corresponds to the logical organization in the mapped data. Color is a complex subject, and, even more so than font choice, it can evoke strong psychological responses. While there isn't room to fit an entire course on color theory in this chapter, we'll look at the basic elements of color and how it impacts the map message, as well as differences in colors for print and digital publications. We'll also learn how to change color models and create custom colors in ArcGIS Pro.

In this chapter, we will cover the following topics:

- Defining color
- Working with color
- Moving beyond the basics

Defining color

As children, we often think of color in terms of crayons, but in reality, color is defined in a number of different ways, depending on the application. In our early experimentation, we learned that red, yellow, and blue combine to make other colors, but that didn't stop us from coveting the box of crayons or colored pencils with some astronomical number of colors to get brightly saturated colors of all shades.

Color models

When we think of color, we tend to think of it in terms of color that has been applied to something, rather than color that is generated by something. When we print images, this is exactly how color works—we apply the colors we want. When we look at images on a screen, however, what we see is colored light, which combines differently to generate those colors. Let's look at these two methods, as well as a few color models used by most software applications, including ArcGIS Pro.

Cyan, Magenta, Yellow, and Black (CMYK)

CMYK is the color model for print, sometimes referred to as four-color process printing, because each color is laid down individually. Our standard blending crayons got an upgrade as CMYK which stands for Cyan, Magenta, Yellow and Black (or Key, depending on which tradition you endorse). If you've ever replaced the ink in a color printer, you'll recognize these names. CMYK color is **subtractive color**, which means that the colored surface absorbs or subtracts everything but the color you see. Subtractive color is what we see all around us—in plants, clothing, paint, and even that box of crayons. In this case, black is created by combining the other three colors, which means everything is being subtracted from the previously white paper. This is why black surfaces are much hotter in sunlight than lighter colors; they are busily absorbing all the colors. In reality, however, combining cyan, magenta, and yellow results in a pretty muddy shade of black, which is why a true black is added to the process. CMYK values are specified in terms of percentages, so each color is represented in values (0, 100). In this format, (100, 0, 0, 0) would be **pure cyan**, (0, 100, 0, 0) would be **pure magenta**, and so on. **Pure white** is (0, 0, 0, 0), and **pure black**, because of the added black (*K*) value, is (0, 0, 0, 100). Shades of gray are obtained by ranging the black value between (0, 100). CMYK values can be readily looked up from a variety of charts available from professional printers, or from web tools like the ones mentioned later in the *Color schemes* section:

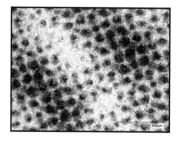

Figure 5.1: CMYK dots at 200 times magnification, CC BY British Library

Red, Green, Blue (RGB)

RGB is the color model used by digital devices, such as your phone, TV, or computer monitor, and which combines to make all other colors. RGB is what is referred to as an additive color mode, which means that all three colors combine to make white. The color that you see is the color that is coming directly into your eye. If you've ever been to a concert or theater performance, you may have noticed that white lights are seldom used, except for the occasional spotlight. Individual beams of red, blue, and green (and sometimes other colors) are directed at key parts of the stage, where they appear more or less white, depending on the levels of each color. Unlike the classic yellow and blue make green in CMYK, in RGB color, green and red combine to make yellow. RGB colors are specified in values in the range of (0, 255), so (255, 0, 0) is **pure red**, (0, 255, 0) is **pure green**, and so forth. **White** is represented as (255, 255, 255) and **black** as (0, 0, 0). Shades of gray are obtained by adjusting all values to the same number. RGB values can also be looked up with a variety of web tools:

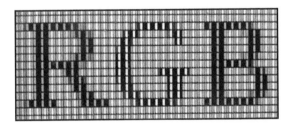

Figure 5.2: Detail of computer monitor, LCD RGB CC BY Luís Flávio Loureiro dos Santos

Hue, Saturation, Value (HSV)

HSV is also sometimes called **Hue**, **Saturation**, **Brightness** (HSB). HSV is also an additive model, like RGB. **Hue** refers to the actual color (red, blue, and many more). **Saturation** is the dilution of the hue with gray. Desaturating, or adding gray to colors, can dramatically impact the feel, or mood, of a map. **Value** is the amount of white or black added to the color, which effectively lightens or darkens it.

HSV is sometimes used as an alternative to RGB in digital color space, as it matches the way most people think about color more closely:

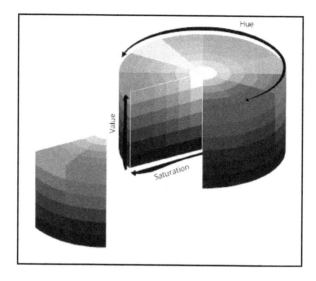

Figure 5.3: HSV model, adapted from HSV Cilindro CC BY Iñaki Ochoa

ArcGIS Pro also includes **Hue**, **Saturation,** and **Lightness** (**HSL**), a variant on HSV, **Grayscale** (shades of gray), and **Lab**, which is composed of absolute color values, rather than combinations of primary colors.

Hexadecimal

Hexadecimal, or hex colors, are the color definitions used by web browsers to deliver specific RGB values. The first two digits represent *red*, the second pair *green*, and the last pair *blue*, each pair with a value from `00` (fully off) to `FF` (fully on). Thus, `#FF0000` would be red fully on, and other colors off, or pure red, and so forth. In this model, `#000000` represents *black* and `#FFFFFF` represents *white*. In ArcGIS Pro, hex codes can be specified with or without the leading # symbol. You can also shorthand hex codes when the digit pairs are identical; `E9C` is identical to `EE99CC`.

Hexadecimal codes can be referenced from a chart (`http://www.color-hex.com/`), through the tools mentioned in the *Color schemes* section, or by using a conversion calculator that converts CMYK or RGB to hex codes. This latter method is not recommended if you are using more than a couple of colors, as it can be quite tedious, and conversions may not translate exactly.

Setting colors in Pro

So, why do we care about all these different color models? After all, ArcGIS Pro can swap between color models with a simple change of settings, right? If you've ever printed off something in color and been frustrated that it doesn't match what's on your screen, you already have a hint of why that's not a great solution. As noted already, while there are conversion tools to hop between methods, they don't match exactly, and sometimes, odd things may happen. It's therefore really quite important to specify your colors in the format that will be used when the map is printed (or delivered digitally). If you're providing it in multiple formats, start with the one that is most critical to get right, usually the print version. For example, if you need to serve a map on your website and also print it in a report, build it in CMYK. Then, create a copy and convert it to RGB or hexadecimal, depending on your needs; then check your colors carefully in the digital version to make sure you're getting what you expect.

To access detailed color settings in ArcGIS Pro, select **Color Properties** from the bottom of the color palette in any place that you're choosing colors. The **Color Editor,** as seen in the following figure, will appear. From here, you can set the **Color Model**, which will change the number of color channels available. Set the color values using the sliders, or type or click the arrows to set a numeric value for each channel (the **Transparency** setting will be discussed in *Color schemes in ArcGIS Pro* section):

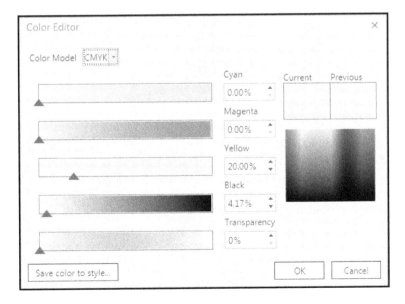

Figure 5.4: ArcGIS Pro Color Editor

Once you've set all the channels for your color, you can save it using **Save color to style...**, so you'll have your custom colors at your fingertips whenever you need them.

Color wheel

The **color wheel** is a tool used to visualize the color spectrum in a way that helps designers make decisions about color combinations. A quick Google search will yield a vast number of variations on the theme, but let's start with a basic 12-color wheel, as shown in the following figure:

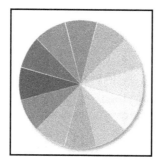

Figure 5.5: A classic color wheel

From this, it is easy to visualize how the primary colors of RGB or **Cyan**, **Magenta**, **Yellow** (**CMY**) blend to form other colors. The color wheel is also helpful for developing color schemes, discussed in the *Color schemes* section.

Warm and cool colors

The color wheel is often broken up into warm and cool colors as a further design aid. **Warm colors** are considered to be the *red* to *yellow* section, and tend to appear to advance visually. These are generally more vivid, even in subdued shades, and can be used to great effect to add importance to small areas, but should be used with caution for secondary items that may appear to be more important than they are if represented in warm colors. **Cool colors** are the *green* to *blue* section. These may appear to recede slightly or be more soothing. German elevation maps use this to great effect by making lowland areas green, and, as elevation increases, moving to vivid oranges. Purple is usually grouped with cool colors, but if it has sufficient red in it, it may act as a warm color, so is often a great compromise color when warms are too intense and cool is too passive.

Complementary colors

Complementary colors are those which appear opposite each other on the color wheel. If you think of the wheel like a clock, this would be *6* and *12*, or *9* and *3*, and many more. These color combinations have special properties and can result in the appearance of color harmonics—the place where the two colors meet may appear to be vibrating slightly, depending on the intensity of the colors. This contrast, or color tension, can easily overwhelm the map message.

Working with color

Applying color to maps is a little more complicated than just picking a few things off the wheel. We have physical and psychological interactions with color, and it's important to understand the basics of these before we start madly coloring in shapes.

Color theory

Color theory is the formalized examination of the blending of colors and how we perceive them. Early 19th century works by Goethe and others documented such phenomena as complementary colors and color afterimages. Evolution in science led to a better understanding of the visual perception of color, and technological advances in chemistry made color printing and photography more feasible, which led to the development of the RGB and CMYK models. From these, and later work on the subject, we came to understand how colors interact with each other, and how the brain interprets those interactions.

To simplify for our purposes, let's look at three basic principles of color:

- Colors interact with their environment; namely, with each other. This simultaneous contrast alters how we perceive each of these colors. In complementary colors, this contrast can be quite pronounced, even painful.
- Our eyes have color memory, which can also impact our perception, by carrying over color from one space to the next. This is sometimes called the **watercolor effect**, where one color bleeds into the next.
- Lines have power. White and black stop the interaction of colors, and small outlines can be used effectively to place colors next to each other that would otherwise suffer from color memory and simultaneous contrast.

Color as a visual variable

Like text, color can be used to represent qualitative and quantitative data on a map. Qualitative schemes are typically best represented with distinct colors, as color values and data values are typically unconnected (with the exception of the cartographic conventions noted earlier). Quantitative schemes may use one or more colors, but, more importantly, vary the value of each color to imply quantity.

Qualitative data is usually represented with categorical colors, where each value has a different hue. Colors selected in this scheme should have equal values, which means no one color should dominate the others in terms of visual hierarchy. Certain colors, such as reds or intense blues, can be difficult to manage in this sort of scheme, unless they are used sparingly. Road maps are a classic example of categorical colors, with red roads, blue rivers, and green parks and forests (as shown in the following figure):

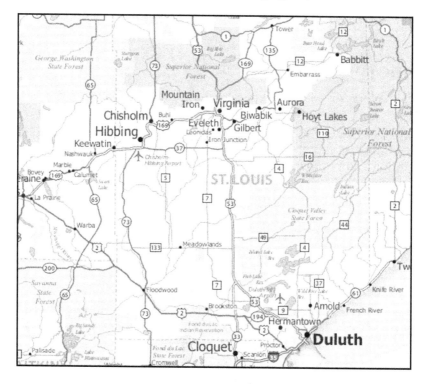

Figure 5.6: Categorical scheme used to distinguish types of features

Categorical colors can also be used to represent data such as soil types, primary exports, or any other dataset where each value, or category, is unrelated to the others numerically. Each color needs to be distinct, but work in harmony with the others. A common beginner's mistake is to select the rainbow palette, which has the advantage of providing many distinct color values, but it has the disadvantage of looking like a unicorn was sick all over your map (as shown in the following figure):

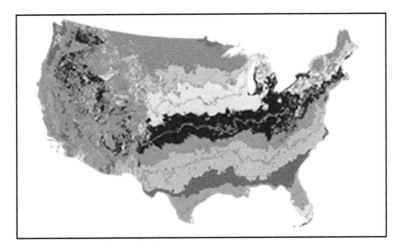

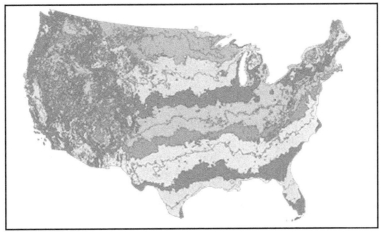

Figure 5.7: Categorical colors should be chosen with care (top), to avoid the sick unicorn effect of the default schemes (bottom)

With quantitative data, the magnitude of the data value is represented by the intensity of the color. One of the most common quantitative color maps is the **choropleth map**. In choropleth maps, boundary units are filled with a solid color, and the pattern of colors reveals the pattern of data. Probably the most familiar choropleth map to US residents is the classic election map trotted out every fall. The following figure shows the classic blue for **Democrats** and red for **Republicans**, with shades of purple representing mixed counties:

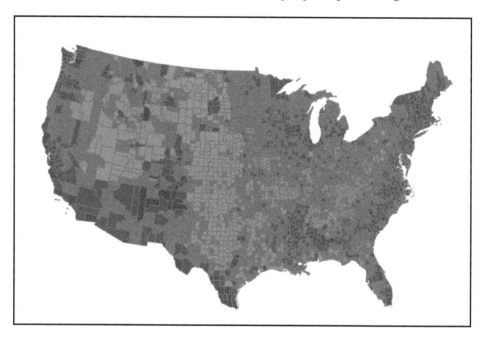

Figure 5.8: Choropleth maps, commonly used for election data

For a single data variable, a **sequential** scheme is best, to help the reader understand that the same data is represented across the map, in varying amounts. In sequential schemes, a single hue is chosen and then varied by value. This makes the map very easy to interpret since it is inferred that darker colors equate to more significant (typically higher) values.

The following figure shows median income, from lowest (light green) to highest (dark green):

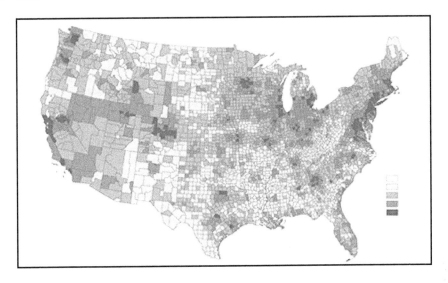

Figure 5.9: Sequential schemes help show an increase in value

Diverging schemes are similar to sequential schemes in that the colors vary in intensity. The key difference is that diverging schemes have a different color at each end of the spectrum, and decrease in value toward a neutral, which typically represents the median value. Divergent schemes are a great way to emphasize the two ends of your data, such as when mapping hot and cool spots, or standard deviation. The following figure shows median income, with purple counties being above average and orange counties below average:

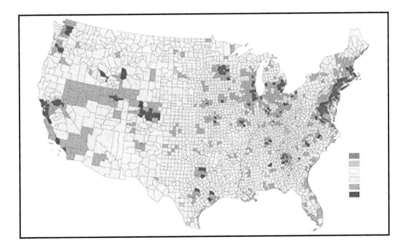

Figure 5.10: Diverging schemes show deviation from a midpoint

Color schemes

Building color schemes can be complicated. You might have a base color or two that you want to include, to either reflect the type of data mapped or coordinate with other graphics in a report or presentation. But where do you go from there? Fortunately, there are a number of online tools to help:

- **Adobe Color CC (formerly Adobe Kuler)**: http://color.adobe.com
- **Paletton (formerly Color Scheme Designer)**: http://paletton.com
- **Color Palette Generator**: http://www.degraeve.com/color-palette
- **Color Brewer**: http://colorbrewer2.org

The first two listed here are great for developing color schemes that really work well, which is particularly useful if you don't have a lot of experience choosing colors, or if you're just not feeling particularly inspired in the moment. The third tool lets you pull color values from an image, which is a great way to match existing graphics. The last tool lets you try out sequential and diverging schemes, as well as restrict choices to colorblind safe palettes. A quick web search will reveal a huge list of other such tools; find one that works for you and bookmark it!

If you've never worked with a tool like **Color CC** or **Paletton** before, some of the terminologies may be a little unfamiliar:

- **Monochromatic:** Monochrome schemes are just like they sound—composed of tints and shades of a single color. These are great for sequential schemes that show the intensity of a variable, as darker or more intense colors imply larger or more concentrated data values, and are therefore very intuitive for the map reader. Monochrome is, of course, also heavily used as grayscale, when we are confined to making maps without color.
- **Analogous:** Sometimes also called **adjacent**, these schemes use colors that are next to each other on the color wheel. In maps, these can help add more classes in a sequential ramp, as more than five shades of a single color can be hard to distinguish. They can also provide subtle distinctions between qualitative variables, such as sub-classes in a soil map, or perhaps weekday/weekend variations of a bus route. They should be used with caution for distinctly separate variables or figure to ground delineations, as there is usually an insufficient contrast to help the viewer interpret the change.

- **Dichromatic**: Again, as the term implies, dichromatic schemes are composed of two colors. This can be two variables arranged as monochromatic schemes, or a diverging scheme with two colors converging toward a neutral center. Dichromatic schemes can be done with two colors near each other, such as red and blue, or complementary colors, such as blue and orange (but remember the special properties of these).

- **Complementary**: As discussed earlier in the *Complementary colors* section, complementary colors are directly opposite to each other and provide a high-contrast effect. If used at full saturation, this can be quite jarring, so it takes a bit of finesse to use this scheme effectively. Many sports teams use complementary colors to generate excitement; think of the blue and orange of the Denver Broncos or the New York Mets, for example, or the purple and yellow of the Minnesota Vikings or the LA Lakers. In maps, however, this can distract from the overall message, so should be carefully managed.

- **Split Complementary**: Split complements use a base color and then the two colors on either side of the complement. These are much easier to manage than the straight complementary scheme, as the harmonics of the contrast are less intense. If we refer back to our clock face example, this might look like 11, 1, and 6, rather than the 12 and 6 of the regular complementary scheme.

- **Triads**: You probably already know where this is going—three colors. Unlike split complements, which are also three colors, triads are spaced evenly around the wheel; think about drawing an equilateral triangle between your clock numbers. For best results, choose one color to dominate, and let the other two provide accents. These schemes are often quite vibrant, even with lighter or desaturated values.

- **Tetrads**: If you know your geometric terms, you'll know this is a four-color scheme, arranged as two complementary pairs. It works best with a balance of warm and cool colors, and can be used either with one dominant color (by desaturating or lightening the others) or for four variables of equal intensity, although the latter should be managed carefully to avoid excess color tension, since you're effectively using two complementary schemes:

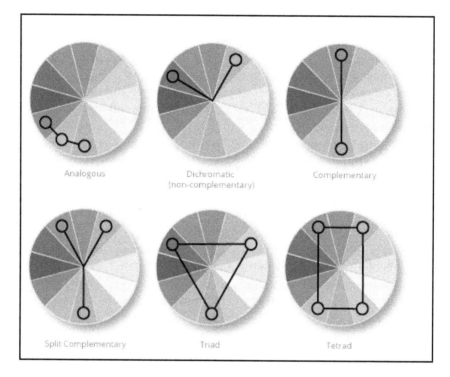

Figure 5.11: Multicolor schemes

Color schemes in ArcGIS Pro

In addition to selecting individual colors, ArcGIS Pro also provides a selection of color schemes (also called color ramps), which you can use as is or customize to suit your needs. Continuous schemes are used with continuous data, such as **Digital Elevation Models** (**DEMs**), hillshades, or other surfaces. Discrete schemes are continuous schemes with specific color stops, great for sequential and diverging schemes in choropleth maps.

Random schemes are good for qualitative datasets and save time when you need an array of colors of similar values. Multi-part schemes are layered ramps composed of continuous, discrete, and/or random ramps. Two ramps can be combined to make a diverging scheme, or multiple ramps (up to 20) can be combined for specialized uses, such as elevation maps.

The default set of color ramps is good for quick visualizations but is seldom what we want for a final product. You can import schemes from other styles, or create your own.

Let's work with some election data and try out some of these options on a basic choropleth map:

1. Start a new **Blank Project** in Pro. Save it as `Chapter5 Samples`.

If you haven't done so already, set your default basemap to **None** (**Project**|**Options**|**Map and Scene**). Unless your organization works with the same map for every project, this is the most efficient setting, so you don't have to remove the Esri basemap every time you start a new map.

2. Download the election map data from the `Chapter 5 data` folder on the website and add it to your map.
3. Set the projection to **USA Albers Equal Area Conic**. When looking at election results, we can compare either areas or population to get the best view of how the votes tally up. Since we're looking at votes by county, in this case, we're comparing areas, and will need to reduce that distortion in our map.
4. Zoom in to the lower 48 states by holding *Shift*, then dragging a box around them. (Sorry, Alaska and Hawaii; we'll get to you in a minute!). Set a bookmark (**Bookmarks**|**New Bookmark**) and call it `lower48`.
5. Take a look at the attribute table. You'll see two columns near the end, **per_dem** and **per_gop**, which represent the percentage of the vote earned by the specified party. Since it's already calculated as a percentage, we won't need to normalize our data, but if we used the **votes_dem** or **votes_gop** columns (which count total votes), we'd need to divide by total votes to make sure we aren't just making a population map.
6. Click on the layer symbol in the **Contents** pane, and in the **Symbology** pane, click the back arrow.
7. Change the **Symbology** to **Graduated Colors** and set the **Field** to **per_dem**.

8. The default **Method** is **Natural Breaks**, but that's not ideal for this sort of data, especially if we want to compare it with the **per_gop** field later. Let's set the class breaks at intervals of 20%:

   1. In the table at the bottom of the pane, set the **Upper values** to **0.2**, **0.4**, **0.6**, **0.8**, and **1.0**
   2. In the upper-right corner, click the **Menu** button and select **Advanced**
   3. Expand **Format Labels** and change the **Category** to **Percentage**
   4. Click the button next to **Number represents a fraction...**
   5. Change the **Decimal places** to **0**
   6. Click the back button. Your settings should look like the following figure:

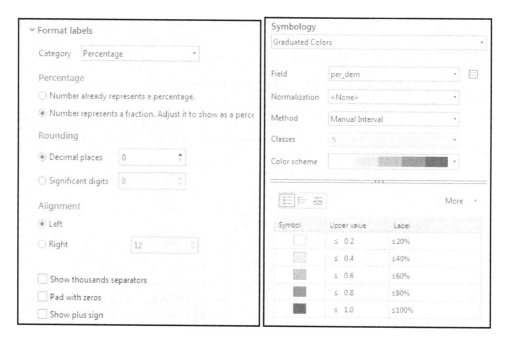

Figure 5.12: Formatting labels and setting interval values

9. From the **Color scheme** drop-down menu, check **Show names**, then scroll to the Blues (5 classes):

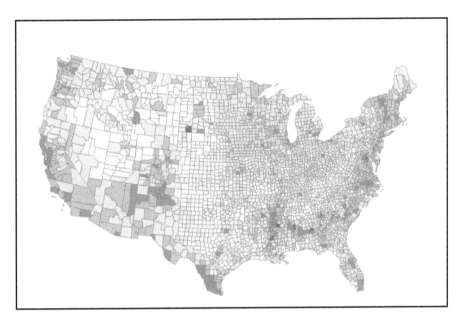

Figure 5.13: Single hue sequential scheme

We've now got a nice sequential color scheme in a single hue. That's not particularly useful for election data, however, when we're essentially looking at the variation between two possible values.

Since the two parties make up the majority of votes, what we really want for this data is a diverging scheme. We can, for the moment, ignore third-party options, and make a quick mock-up of what the overall results look like:

1. In the **Color scheme** drop-down menu, check **Show All**. Scroll to Red-Blue (5 classes).
2. Make sure that the red values are at the lower end (0-40%) of the **per_dem** values, and the blues are at the upper end. If that's not the case, click the **More** button and **Reverse values**.

3. Now we've got a rough approximation of the maps plastered all over the news following the election:

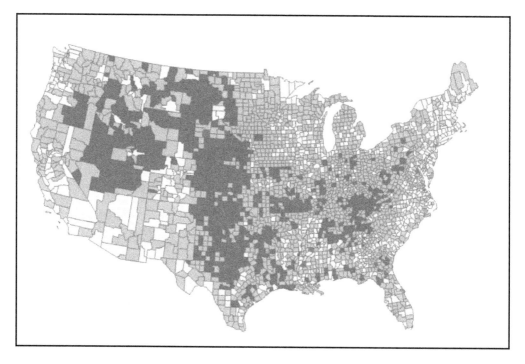

Figure 5.14: Diverging scheme

But this really implies a strong rift between parties, with a bunch of neutral counties, when it might be more accurate to represent the middle values as they are—a blend of voters, blue and red:

1. Set the **Color scheme** back to Blues (5 classes)
2. In the **Contents** pane, copy the election layer, and then paste it
3. In this new layer, change the **Field** to **per_gop** and the **Color scheme** to Reds (5 classes)
4. Repeat the process from earlier to set upper values and format the labels
5. On the **Appearance** tab, set the **Transparency** slider to **70%**.

Now, the blue layer shows through the red and renders a number of counties in something more like purple. It's not a very good purple, because the blues and reds used to represent the parties aren't the traditional shades, either. That middle red shade is pretty orange-looking, and the blues are largely desaturated, leaving a gray haze over the map:

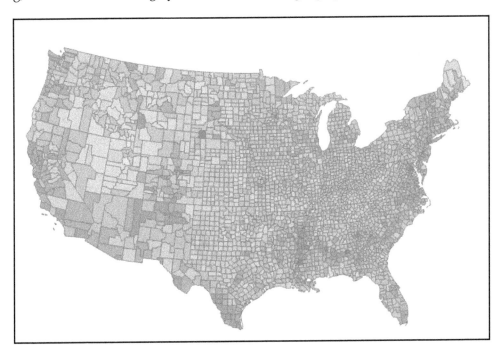

Figure 5.15: Layered sequential schemes with top layer transparency

Let's do a little color correction. Discrete ramps, like we're using now, are established by setting color stops, sometimes called crayons, along the way, to set each color individually. To change the overall color family, we'd have to set each crayon individually:

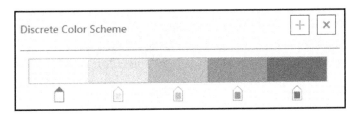

Figure 5.16: Discrete color scheme showing color stops, or crayons

Continuous single-color ramps can be built with a color stop at each end, and then use a blending algorithm to set the intervening colors, which means that we only have to set a start and end color and let the computer do the work, and that we are less likely to pick a shade that doesn't quite flow:

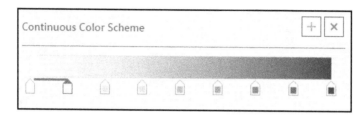

Figure 5.17: Continuous color scheme, showing blending between color stops

1. For your **per_dem** layer, click the **Color scheme** drop-down menu and select Blues (continuous). Click the drop-down menu again and select **Format color scheme**.
2. Click the second crayon from the left, and then click the **X** over the bar to remove it (be careful not to click the **X** that closes the **Color Scheme Editor**).
3. Keep clicking the **X** until all crayons are gone except the first and last ones. You'll probably notice the color ramp shifting slightly as you go.
4. Click the left-hand crayon and set the **Color** to White. Since White is already on the palette, you can select it from there.
5. Click the right-hand crayon, and this time, we'll set the color to a nice, political blue. At the bottom of the palette, select **Color Properties**.
6. Set the **Color model** to **RGB** and then set the RGB values to (0, 0, 230), respectively. This should be a nice, bright blue.
7. Click **Save color to style...** and name it Democrat Blue.
8. Click **OK**. Admire your new color ramp.
9. Click **Save to a style** and name it Dem Ramp.
10. Click **OK** again to apply it to your map.
11. Repeat the process for your **per_gop** layer. Set the left crayon to white and the right crayon to RGB (240, 0, 0). Save the color as GOP Red and the ramp as GOP Ramp.

At this point, you may find that the red areas are a little pink-peach colored, so turn the **Transparency** back down to about **50%**. You should now have much better purples, and less dull-looking colors overall:

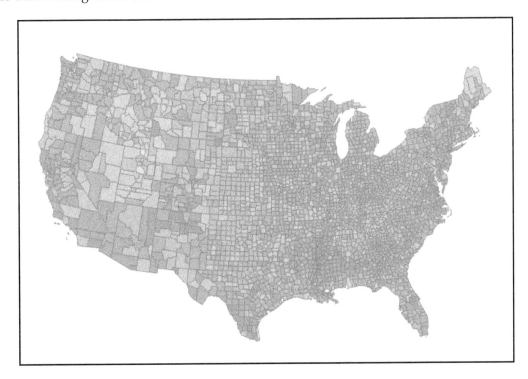

Figure 5.18: Custom colors improve the look

While this is definitely less dull, and the purple areas make us look less polarized as voters, it's lacking the strong reds and blues of the high percentage counties, and the whole thing looks a little foggy.

Go back in and edit your red and blue ramps. This time, instead of white for the left crayon, select **No Color**.

Now we've got some purple stuff, but also some bright reds and blues in those high percentage counties. Since we've got the transparency built into the ramps, you can turn down the **Transparency** in the **per_gop** layer; about **25%** gives a nice result in the purple areas:

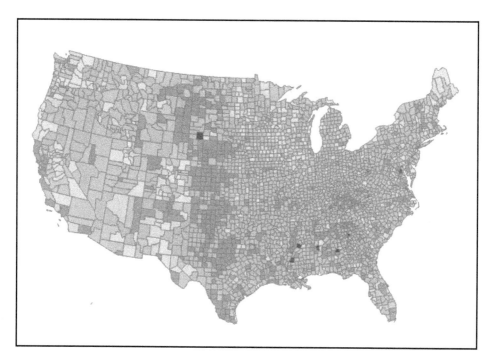

Figure 5.19: Adding transparency to ramps instead of layers

ArcGIS Pro also has two different algorithms for blending color ramps. You can find these in the **Color Scheme Editor,** right under the color settings. CIELab blends two colors without crossing through intervening colors; rather than travel around the wheel, it takes the shortest path, which can result in a smoother transition. This method does sometimes result in muddy centers when the two end colors are far apart on the wheel. **HSV** travels in a linear path around the wheel, blending through all intervening colors, including saturation and value settings. This is perhaps more intuitive when thinking about how the colors are blended, but can result in some hard -to-read map results. The default setting is **CIELab**, which you can generally leave as is, unless you are having trouble resolving those muddy centers.

Importing schemes

While the basic ramps included in ArcGIS Pro can be disappointing, other ramps can be loaded in quite easily, rather than having to recreate them yourself. Esri has published a great set of color ramps for doing elevation and bathymetry, but they have other uses, as well. You can find them embedded in a blog post at: `https://blogs.esri.com/esri/arcgis/2011/12/17/esri-color-ramps-version-30/`. It's the first link in the post.

Download the `ColorRamps3.0.zip` file from Esri and unzip it into your folder. You can put it directly into the `Styles` folder, or anywhere you will have access to it when you need it (such as a server drive):

1. In ArcGIS Pro, open an existing project, or start a new one.
2. On the **Insert** ribbon, click **Import** from the **Styles** section.
3. Browse to where you saved the `ColorRamps3.0` folder and double-click to show the ramps in that folder.
4. Click on the ramps you wish to install (hold *Shift* to click multiples).
5. Click **OK**. The ramps will now be included in your **Color scheme** drop-down menu for this project. You'll need to add them again if you want to use them in another project.

Migrating from ArcMap? You can import styles from ArcMap using this same process. Browse to your `ArcGIS Desktop` folder under `Program Files (x86)` and look for the `Styles` folder. The **Real Estate** style has some great, subtle color ramps, good for hillshades when they're not the focus of the map. You also don't need to recreate your ramps from scratch; just import your saved styles from wherever you saved them.

Color as accent

Sometimes, you might not want a full-color map, but rather a black-and-white or grayscale map with just a splash of color. You might be asking, "Why would I limit myself?" For print publications, costs can often be reduced by printing in black and white with a single added color, called a **spot color**. In addition, a tiny amount of accent color can really pop your data off the page. An early example is this cholera map of **Exeter**, compiled by Thomas Shapter in the 19th century.

The rather gruesome subject jumps off the map, with the only color being the red bars representing deaths:

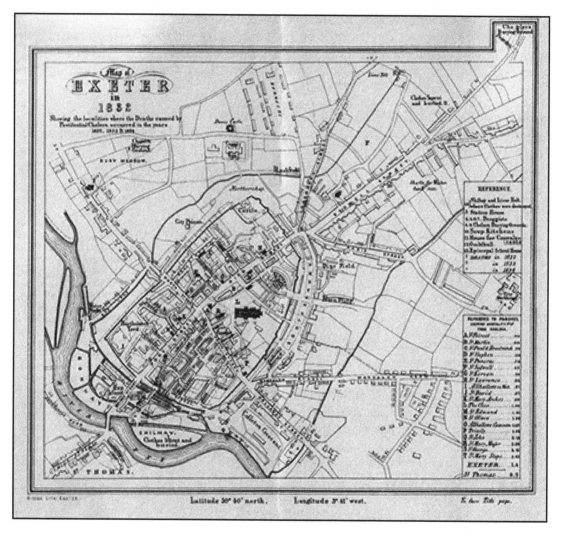

Figure 5.20: Frontispiece, The History of the Cholera in Exeter in 1832 CC BY SA 3.0 C. Risdon

It can be tricky to do this well. Too much, and you may disrupt your sense of hierarchy. Too little, and it looks like you just forgot to convert one of your layers to grayscale. The best approach is to think about your overall hierarchy, and give those top-tier items a little boost. If you're adding color to something in the second tier, you've moved beyond accent color into a color map. For accent color to have the best impact, you should generally use just one color (two, in rare circumstances) and think carefully about adding color to more than two things.

Moving beyond the basics

So far, we've looked at some fairly basic applications of color in maps, coloring single features or adding a simple ramp to choropleth data. But sometimes we want to go beyond the basic and make a map that's slightly more sophisticated in the way color represents the data, sets a mood, or works with patterns.

Value-by-alpha

Value-by-alpha is a technique developed by cartographers Robert Roth, Andy Woodruff, and Zach Johnson, to enable the inclusion of a second variable relating to size. Traditionally, this has been done with cartograms. This technique involves distorting the size of an area, such as states or counties, to represent their share of some variable, such as population. The **value-by-alpha** technique is generally easier for map readers to interpret, as it preserves the expected size and shape of the area, and instead expands upon the *darker equals more* concept that map readers already interpret intuitively. Let's go back to that diverging scheme and make some adjustments. Instead of transitioning through white, we want that center value to be a nice blend of the red and blue:

1. Change the ramp to a **Continuous scheme**, then remove all of the crayons except the one on each end.
2. If you saved your individual colors earlier (not just the ramp), set the left crayon to **GOP Red** and the right crayon to **Dem Blue**. (If you didn't save them, the RGB values are (240, 0, 0) and (0, 0, 230)). They should blend through a nice, vibrant purple in the middle.

3. Click **OK** and see how many formerly blue and red areas are now purple, representing the mix of voters in those counties:

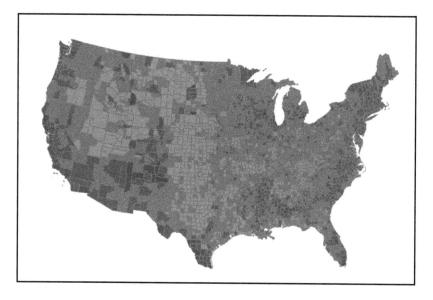

Figure 5.21: Blended color scheme

This is better, but it still misrepresents counties, in that they all appear to have equal weight. Some counties are very densely populated, while others are sparsely populated. To get a true sense of where the votes are, we can add another layer effect, called value-by-alpha, which will adjust the visibility of this layer based on the population density of the counties:

4. Right-click and copy the election layer and paste it into the map.
5. Change the **Field** to **POP08_SQMI** and change the **Method** to **Geometric Interval**.
6. Select either the **Democrat** or **Republican** color ramp, and then click the drop-down menu again and select **Format color scheme**.
7. Set both end crayons to white (if there are any stops in between, remove them). This resets the color memory in the middle section.
8. Leave the left stop white and set the right to **No Color**.
9. You should now have a white-to-transparent ramp. Click **Save to style** and save it as `Value by Alpha`. Click **OK** twice.

Your map should now have an overlay of white to clear that lets counties with high population density show through, and low-density counties are masked out. This gives a much different view of how votes are distributed. Since there are actual voters in those masked out counties, you can set the **Transparency** for the whole layer to **10%** to let them show through slightly:

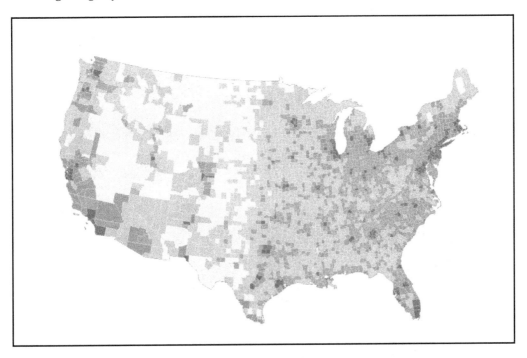

Figure 5.22: Adding a value-by-alpha layer to mask votes by population density

To make a legend for these types of maps, you'll need to arrange them so the color swatches are stacked on top of each other, then ungroup the legend and manually clean up the swatch labels.

Sophisticated spot color

If you're not restricted to printing with true spot color, but still want the impact of isolated color on a neutral background, you can do some pretty amazing things with layered transparent fills. John Nelson of Esri has used this to spectacular effect in several maps, with what he refers to as *Firefly cartography*:

Figure 5.23: Firefly mapping technique by John Nelson. Used with permission.

This technique uses the impact of spot color, but with layer upon layer of transparent symbols, which not only draws the eye right to the data, but gives an immediate impression of the magnitude of the variable. John shows off this technique in his blog at: `https://adventuresinmapping.com/2017/11/01/earthquakes-and-emergence/`, and provides a complete tutorial at: `https://blogs.esri.com/esri/arcgis/2017/10/26/luminance-hack/`, along with the fuzzy little gradient images he uses to create the halos.

Color moods

The significance of certain colors is highly cultural. For example, in the US, black is a color traditionally associated with funerals and death, but in other cultures, white is the color for mourning. Red can mean danger or fire, but it may also signify happiness and prosperity. These guidelines are presented largely from a Western perspective; make sure you know your map audience when establishing mood.

Some common color associations:

- **Blue**: Water, cool, positive numerical values, serenity, depression, melancholy, truth, purity, formality, depth, restraint, loneliness
- **Green**: Vegetation, lowlands, forests, youth, spring, nature, envy, greed, jealousy, cheap, ignorance, peace
- **Red**: Warm, important items (roads, cities), action, life, blood, fire, heat, passion, danger, power, loyalty, bravery, anger, excitement, warning
- **Yellow/Tan**: Dryness, lack of vegetation, intermediate elevations, hot, cheerful, dishonest, youth, light, hate, cowardice, joy, optimism, spring, strong, warning
- **Orange**: Harvest, fall, abundance, fire, attention, action, warning
- **Brown**: Landforms (mountains, hills), contours, cozy, dull, reassuring
- **Purple**: Dignity, royalty, sorrow, despair, richness, elegant
- **White**: Purity, clean, faith, illness
- **Black**: Mystery, strength, heaviness
- **Grays**: Quiet, reserved, sophisticated, controlled

Note that some of these have geographic references in them. These tie in with other cartographic conventions and should be remembered when mapping in color. For example, blue should not be used for anything but water if there is water on your map. Making a map of hot and cold spots for a particular phenomenon? Feel free to use a blue and red color scheme; just make sure you leave off any lakes and rivers that fall inside your mapped area. In general, the conventions follow natural colors—green for vegetation, blue for water, and browns and yellows for bare earth or landform indicators, like contour lines.

Color acuity

Not everyone sees color in the same way, and as designers of a visual product, we need to take that into account. Around 8% of men and less than 1% of women have some degree of color blindness. Red-green is the most common, but there are other variations, as well. As mapmakers, we have to be especially aware of color, as we often use it to encode features. Red-green color ramps are frequently used to represent positive and negative values of some variable, and may be difficult to distinguish. Red and green bus routes, red text on green fill colors; the list goes on. For those who are not color-blind, this may seem like a great combination: complementary colors with high contrast. But for those with decreased acuity, everything may look the same, rendering our map useless.

Color blindness was always challenging to describe for those who have it, and difficult to imagine for those who don't. A quick way to check print maps for acuity issues is to print them on a black and white printer and look for value distinctions in the shades of gray, but this doesn't accurately represent how people with color blindness actually see color. Another tool, which provides a better approximation, is the **Color Blindness Simulator**, at: http://www.color-blindness.com/coblis-color-blindness-simulator/. This tool also lets you check for varying kinds of deficiency, so you can test your map under a variety of conditions. The **Color Brewer tool** features a color-blind safe setting, which will limit scheme choices to those proven to be distinguishable regardless of color acuity.

Do you always need to use color-blind safe colors? No, but you should always take a moment to think about your audience. If you're designing for public meetings or news media, there's a good chance someone who views your map will have trouble if you use red-green ramps. Developing a website map that needs to be accessibility compliant? You should absolutely use color-blind safe colors.

I recommend testing your own acuity, as well, as we often have areas where we are less able to distinguish between subtleties in colors. The color test challenge located at: http://www.xrite.com/online-color-test-challenge, is not a substitute for professional testing, but is a quick, fun way to understand how you see color. At the end, you'll get a report that tells you where you have strong acuity, and areas where your ability to distinguish shades is weaker. For example, you might have some deficiency in the green areas, and select two shades of green that look subtly different to you, but which in fact contrast unpleasantly for people with full acuity. To avoid these issues, work with other areas of the color wheel, and when you must use green in your map, use one of the color scheme tools to let the software calculate the best choices.

Practice on your own

Add two more maps to your project—one for Alaska, and another one for Hawaii; then, add all three maps to a layout.

Summary

In this chapter, we looked at how color is created and perceived, and how to harness it to improve our maps, not just make them colorful. We also took a few basic techniques and upgraded them using Pro's improved transparency handling. At the end of the day, however, it's not about whether or not you chose attractive colors, but whether or not it enhanced the readability of your map. Any time you apply color, it should be helping your message, not hindering it.

In the next chapter, we'll look at further improving map communication through cartographic abstraction. We'll examine the relationship between scale, accuracy, and legibility, and learn ways to aggregate spatial data for maximum impact. For further information, you may refer to Robert E. Roth, Andrew W. Woodruff, Zachary F. Johnson, *Value-by-alpha maps: An alternative technique to the cartogram, The Cartographic Journal, Vol. 47, No. 2,* May 2010 (`https://www.ncbi.nlm.nih.gov/pmc/articles/PMC3173776/?`).

6
All Maps Are Approximations of Reality

Maps can paint a pretty accurate view of our world or data, but there is a common reality of all maps: they are all incorrect. The world is in a constant state of change—rivers ebb and flow, things get built or destroyed, businesses open and close, people migrate, and the earth moves beneath our feet. This constant flux makes keeping track of everything time consuming and costly, but that is sometimes necessary. For most maps, using exact coordinates, displaying complex borders, and labeling every feature is not necessary. In this chapter, you will learn about the general types of maps, how to properly generalize data, and make your data stand out and easy to read.

In this chapter, we will cover the following topics:

- The different styles of maps
- Changing data to make more it more legible
- Aggregating data

Determining the style of your map

The abundance of data in the world today is wonderful; GPS-enabled phones, APIs, open data portals, and cheap IoT devices can give us a wealth of information. Up until now, it was rare to deal with such data-rich content, so the average GIS user didn't need to know how to deal with this abundance. Cartographers for a long time have been working on how to best show data on a map.

In the previous chapters, you learned how to properly choose the right design, colors, and typeface for your map document. In this chapter, we will discuss the purpose of different genres of maps and how to choose which one to use. We will discuss when it's appropriate to change the data to make the map more visually appealing or accessible. We will then close the chapter learning different ways to aggregate and faithfully represent data.

Better understanding of your map

A mapmaker's goal is transfer knowledge to the map's viewer. When someone looks at a map, they are looking for information. This information could be notational or extremely important to them, but the viewer must be able to understand the data quickly. One of the signs of a good map is when it is structured well and can be understood quickly. This doesn't mean the viewer is able to take in every piece of data quickly, it means that they understand the structure of the data and how to interpret it quickly when needed. When creating a new map, there's no need to reinvent the wheel; people have been looking at maps for a while and they are used to specific styles of maps. To better understand how to properly display our data, let's determine what style of map we are going to create. Maps generally fall into three broad categories:

- Reference maps
- Thematic maps
- Special purpose maps

Reference maps

Reference maps generally show many layers of point, line, polygon, and raster data. They focus on the location, and each layer of data is treated equally. Data on reference maps can be simple or complex and can vary in size. The data shown in a reference map is done in such a way that it shows where features are spatially related to each other. The following is an example of a **United States Geological Survey** (**USGS**) quadrangle topographic map:

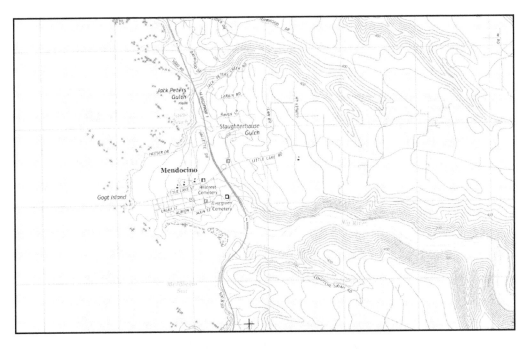

Figure 6.1: USGS topographic map

In *Figure 6.1*, you can see many layers—schools, fire stations, roads, contours, forest boundaries, and a grid. When you look at the data in the map, not one feature is predominately shown. The size changes in the text labels are subtle enough to not draw attention to their difference, but you can see the difference. Other examples of reference maps are foldable road maps, atlases, and online mapping services.

Thematic maps

As the name suggests, thematic maps show a specific theme or topic. These maps generally show quantitative or qualitative data about an area. These maps focus on the distribution of data based on its location. Thematic maps typically show spatial patterns and can be used to compare datasets. There are four general types of thematic maps:

- Dot density
- Proportional symbol
- Isopleth
- Choropleth

Dot density maps show points of data where they lie on the ground. Each data point is drawn even if they overlap. The following is a very early example of a dot density map. It's a map made by Dr. Snow to show cases of cholera near Broad Street in London, England in 1854:

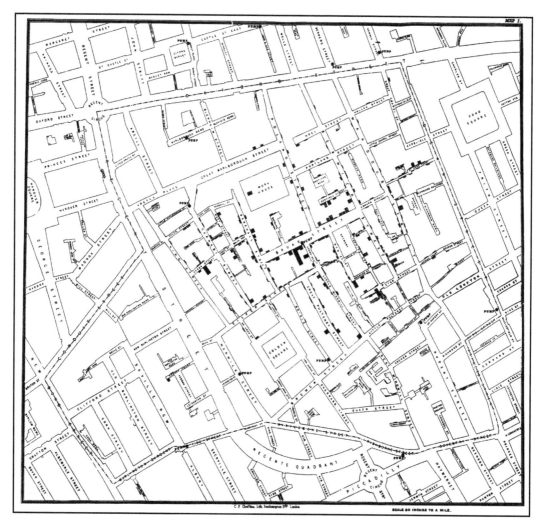

Figure 6.2: Cholera map

Proportional symbol maps show data values by sizing a single symbol based on the data value of a point. These are typically simple maps because it's hard to show multiple datasets with proportional symbols as they will most likely overlap each other. However, you can show multiple attributes of a single point. One example of this is using a pie chart to show the racial makeup of a city and then size the pie chart based on the total population. The following map is a single attribute and multiple attribute proportional symbol maps:

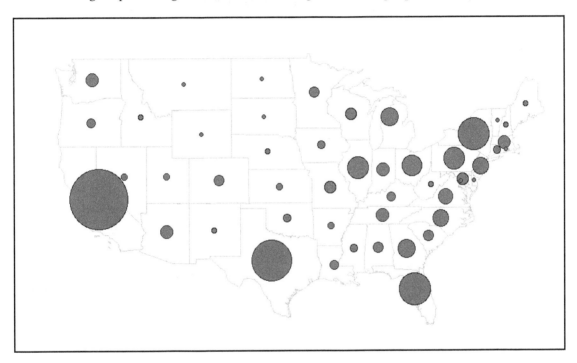

Figure 6.3: Proportional symbol map

Isopleth maps show continuous line data such as elevation or air pressure. These lines are called **isolines**. Each isoline is drawn so that all values on one side are higher or lower than the values on the other side. You can fill the areas between the isolines with a color gradient or leave them blank based on the style of map you are trying to create. The following map shows barometric pressure using isolines:

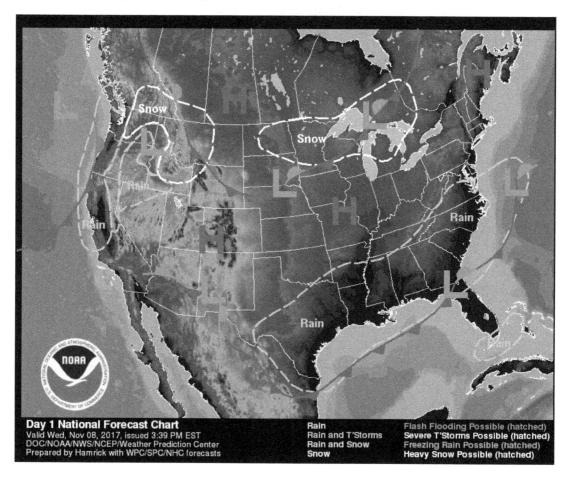

Figure 6.4: Isoline map

Choropleth maps are probably the most popular type of map today. Choropleth maps show quantitative or qualitative data using geographic areas. You display this quantitative or qualitative data by shading the area with color or filling it with a pattern. We will see two examples of a choropleth map. The following map shows the population total for the US, which is the quantitative data of the areas:

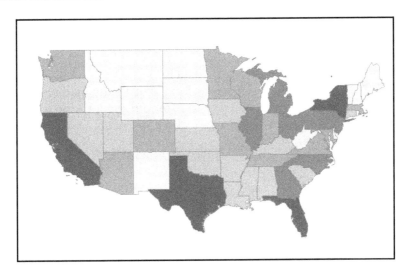

Figure 6.5: Choropleth map

The following map shows the land use categories for a town, which is the qualitative data of the areas:

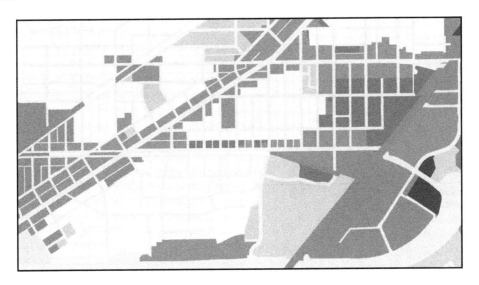

Figure 6.6: Choropleth map of zoning in Sacramento, CA

Special purpose maps

Special purpose maps fall somewhere between reference and thematic maps as they are used to show a specific theme of data while also including reference data typically found in reference maps. These maps are very focused and are specifically made for a very narrow audience. Examples of these are navigational charts used by sailors and pilots or a map of fire roads for wilderness firefighters. Take a look at the following map:

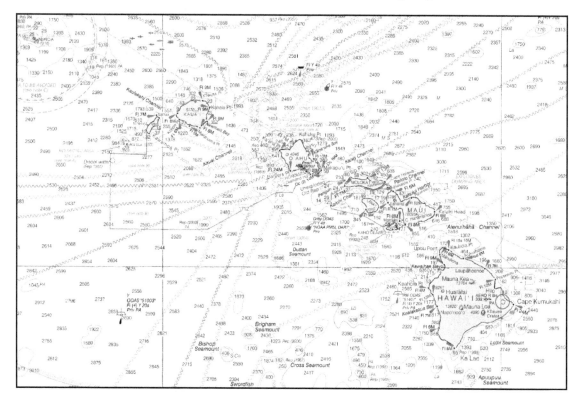

Figure 6.7: Nautical chart

Maybe changing it a little will help make it clearer

As faithful data stewards, GIS users try to keep their data untouched from the source we got it from. Changing data makes the data inaccurate, which will make the map that uses it inaccurate. This is a noble stance, but it is not necessary for a lot of maps. In fact, making the data spatially inaccurate will sometimes allow viewers to better interpret the data and most of the time faster too. A world-famous example of when legibility is prioritized over accuracy is Harry Beck's London Underground Tube map:

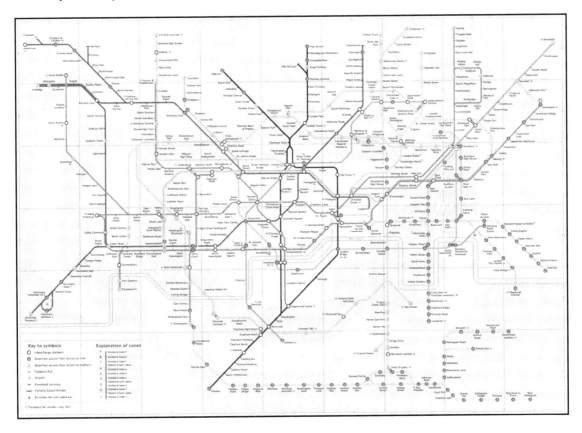

Figure 6.8: London Underground Tube map

This map, while inaccurate spatially to the real world, clearly and effectively shows the data and allows the viewer to easily determine which trains are needed to get to their destination. Having the linear features of the map make bends at 45° angles makes it easier for the viewer to understand and follow the features than understanding them if they came in at multiple angles. While it's rare that you will have to generalize your data to the degree Harry Beck did, as a mapmaker, you can use a cartographic license to make your data more legible. In this section, we will focus on a few ways of generalizing data to increase legibility without a huge hit to spatial accuracy.

Reducing noise

In the last couple of years, people are getting more accustomed to being shown data. The amount of that data is increasing and more products today come with analytics. Having a lot of data can be great, but in mapping, it can become problematic really quickly. Just because you can put more data on your map doesn't mean you have to. Less can be more in mapping. This doesn't mean you keep the layer count small, it just means that you don't want to call attention to all your data layers. For the next couple of sections, we will run through a few exercises where you will have to use noise reduction techniques to make your map more legible while still being faithful to the original data.

To default basemap or not to default basemap

With ArcGIS Pro, Esri gives you a selection of default basemaps to help reduce the amount of work needed to create a map. This can be a great resource to mapmakers but creates an issue—you don't have much control over what is shown in the basemap. The typical default basemap is the topographic basemap. While Esri went to great lengths to create a visually appealing map that can stand on its own, showing data on top of this can be difficult. The following map is an example of the topographic basemap in the island of Manhattan:

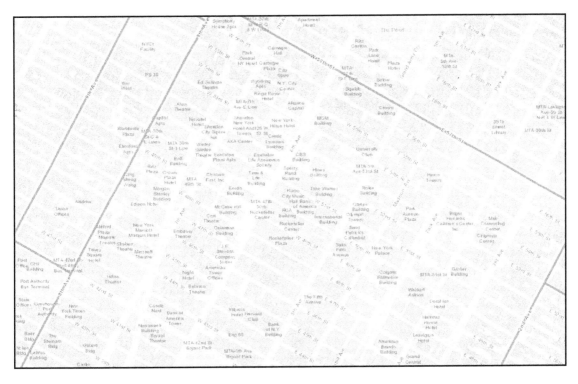

Figure 6.9: Esri topographic basemap

There is a lot going on in this basemap—streets, building footprints of different colors, parks, and pedestrian routes with labels all around. By itself, it tells the viewer a lot, but if you put data on top of it all, these features and labels are going to distract the map viewer and reduce the effectiveness of the map. Also, the usefulness of the labels diminishes if you can't move the labels when your data covers them. The dark gray and light gray basemaps available from Esri help with the feature and label overload of the topographic basemap. These two styles of maps reduce the labeling and features to allow you to better visualize your data but still have the problem of not being able to remove or move labels. For a cleaner cartographic product, making your own basemap can do wonders to the visual appeal of your map. Creating your own basemap will allow you to have full control of your symbology and labeling. With the wealth of GIS data out in the world today, it is easy to find the data you need for a basemap. In the next section, you will learn about a way of making basemap features a little easier on the eyes.

Generalizing boundaries

When making thematic maps, the data we use for reference can actually draw the viewer's eye from the data we, as mapmakers, want to show them. A lot of boundaries that mapmakers use as a basemap can distract viewers from the main purpose of the map. Unless it is specifically needed, you should generalize the boundaries within your basemap. For example, see the following figure:

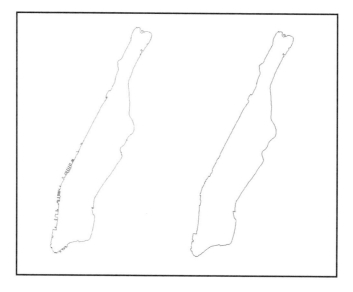

Figure 6.10: Manhattan island outline comparison

The first boundary on the left shows the island of Manhattan with every pier and a little bit of land around the edge of the island. When a map viewer first looks at this, they will most likely notice all the piers along the south-west side of the island. The line work is also very jagged and doesn't look very clean. This will distract our viewer from the data you will show in the map. Using the *Reshape* tool, you can easily cut off the piers in the feature. The result of doing this is the boundary on the right of the figure. This boundary has a lot less noise and looks cleaner. However, there are still a few bumps and jagged areas that need to be cleaned up to make the boundary look clean. To smooth out the boundary, we will use the *Smooth Polygon* tool.

The Smooth Polygon tool is a great cartographic tool that allows us to quickly smooth out a jagged polygon to make it more visually appealing and be less of a distraction to your data. The Smooth Polygon tool has two options for smoothing out a polygon:

- **Polynomial Approximation with Exponential Kernel** (**PAEK**): This method smooths polygons based on a tolerance you define. This tool will create a polygon using straight line vertices that will reshape the polygon only as far as the tolerance you set. Typically, this tool will increase the vertex count in your polygon, so be aware that it could impact the drawing performance of your polygon.
- **Bezier Interpolation**: This method smooths polygons without you setting a tolerance. It will smooth polygons by changing the polygon from many straight line vertices to Bezier curves. Bezier curves are smooth curves that, unlike a straight line and vertex curve, scale indefinitely. This means no matter how far you zoom into a Bezier curve, you won't see the sharp corners a straight line or a vertex curve has.

The choice between the PAEK and Bezier smoothing methods depends on a few factors as each will generate different types of outputs. The following are some of the positives and negatives of each method:

PAEK method	Bezier method
• This can be controlled, so inaccuracies can be managed • This increases the vertex count, increasing the complexity of the polygon and increasing the file size of your feature • This can be exported to a shapefile for use in other programs • When zooming in close to the boundary of your polygon, you will notice jagged curves • This makes it easier to move vertices to reshape the boundary	• This had no controls, so inaccuracies cannot be managed without a complete review and editing • This creates Bezier curves throughout the entire polygon, which reduces the vertex count and reduces the file size of your feature • Shapefiles cannot store Bezier curves and some legacy software cannot use Bezier curves • Bezier curves can scale infinitely, so you will never see jagged edges like you would see in the PAEK method • This makes it harder to reshape the boundary afterward

Now armed with this information, you have a clearer understanding of the difference between both the methods. For this exercise, we will use the *PAEK* method as the polygon complexity isn't very high and we may want to change the polygon border more in the future. To smooth our polygon, refer to our ArcGIS Pro document, `Chapter6.aprx`, and navigate to the **Smooth Polygon** tab. In this map tab, we have the polygon of the island of Manhattan with the piers and small bits of land sticking out. We will want to bring up the **Geoprocessing** pane to access the Smooth Polygon tool. If the **Geoprocessing** pane is not up, navigate to the top **Menu** bar and click on **Tools** under the **Analysis** tab. In the **Search** box in the **Geoprocessing** pane, type in `Smooth Polygon` and hit **Search**. Smooth Polygon (cartography tools) should be the first result. Click on the tool to bring up the tool parameters:

1. For **Input Features**, select **ManhattanNoPiers**
2. For **Output Feature Class**, type `ManhattanNoPiersSmooth` in the default file geodatabase `Chapter6.gdb`
3. Select **Polynomial Approximation with Exponential Kernel** as the smoothing algorithm
4. Set **Smoothing Tolerance** to **50** feet
5. Leave **Preserve endpoints for rings** checked
6. Set **Handling Topological Errors** to **Do not check for topological errors**
7. Click on **Run** to start smoothing the polygon

After a few seconds, you should have your new smoothed polygon. Take a little time to compare the two polygons to see the differences. Make sure that you set **Fill Color** to **No Color** so you can compare the outlines of each polygon.

Labeling

When creating a map, one of the hardest and most tedious tasks is the placing of labels. Labels are important, as not every map viewer is going to understand what some features are or what they represent.

When **labeling**, you want to remind yourself that less is more when mapping. Not every street, park, or political boundary needs to be labeled. The question you should ask yourself is, does the viewer need to know what this feature is for the purpose of my map? If it is a reference map you are creating, you will want more labels as the viewer will be using your map to understand the area of interest. For thematic maps, you would want to minimize the labeling of your basemap as the data is more important. You may need to label your data in certain places and you want to make sure that those labels are not drowned out by other labels.

Scale of your data

An important factor in displaying your data is to fully understand the scale at which it will be presented. As discussed in this chapter, there is an abundance of data nowadays. Mapping all of this dense data can be tough, especially when the data is clumped together and is spread out over a large area. When dealing with so much data, you should fit your map to make sure it captures the entirety of your data. You should also realize that you may need to create an inset map showing a zoomed in portion where the data is too bunched to be seen at the zoom level of your map. Alternatively you may have to aggregate your data so the map viewer can understand it.

Normalizing data

Densely packed data usually needs to be aggregated. Aggregating data can cause a lot of mapping faux pas when not done correctly. Heat maps are a popular type of thematic maps where you aggregate data, but most are not normalized. **Normalizing data** is the process of dividing your data by a value like population or area to minimize differences in your data. Demographic data is a popular type of quantitative data that is used in mapping and can lead to incorrect assumptions or results when displaying data. For example, when looking at demographic data, it is typically denser where the population density is higher. If you don't normalize the data with a value such as population, all your map is going to show is population density.

Aggregating data

As we discussed in this chapter, less is more. However, sometimes this is difficult when you have large amounts of geographically small data such as points or small polygons. When you have this kind of data, it is too much information at the scale you want to present your map in. In the `Chapter6.aprx` project, in the **Uber Points Map** tab, we have a point file of all Uber pickups in Manhattan, NY during June 2014. There is a total of 516,029 points on the island of Manhattan, and many overlap each other. It is almost impossible to show all these points in a meaningful way. Using the default symbology in ArcGIS Pro, we cannot apply anything underneath the layer. If you change the symbology to be a simple 1 pt black dot, you can see some density differences, but it is still not very clear. The small dots show the shape of the street network, which makes sense since Uber pickups are on the side of the street. However, we want to show the density of the data over the whole island with a color ramp so the viewer can easily see the true density of the data.

Aggregation methods

Like many things in GIS, there are many ways of aggregating data. The most common of these aggregation methods are as follow:

- Boundary
- Heat map
- Grid
- Hex bin

While each of these methods are used to simplify large amounts of data for easier readability for the viewer, each has its strengths and weaknesses. Let's look at each method and discuss how best to utilize them.

Boundary

Aggregation by boundary is one of the most commonly used methods of aggregating data. The United States Census uses *blocks*, *block groups*, and *tracts to aggregate data collected in their surveys*. The way the Census department has set up these divisions is to generally have the same amount of population in each. In the case of tracts, each tract is drawn so that they are homogenous relative to population characteristics, meaning that the population inside of a tract is more closely related to each other than those in another tract. While this is not perfect, it gives a best effort in grouping populations. You can also use other boundaries such as counties, districts, states, or countries to aggregate your data.

Heat map

Heat maps have grown in popularity over the years because they are an easy and visually appealing way of showing data. However, the true purpose of a heat map is to show a continuous surface value. The surface created for a heat map will interpolate data in areas where there is no data to keep a continuous surface. For some applications, this is necessary, while it can be misleading in others. A heat map showing temperature is common because there are no areas in that map that will not have a temperature. There may not be any observations in an area, but that doesn't mean that there isn't a temperature there. A heat map will interpolate the values between two observations to give an estimate where there is no data. A good rule of thumb when determining when to use a heat map is whether or not the subject of your data is continuous without breaks.

Grid

A grid or **fishnet** map is a basic way of aggregating data into equal areas across your map. It is a method that has been used for a long time as it is easy on the eyes and is easy for the viewer to understand patterns that show up. You would use a grid map to show non-continuous data over an area where each data point has no influence on the other. While a grid is easy to make and understand, it creates a problem in sampling data. The corners of a cell in a grid are further away from the center of the cell than the midpoint of the side of a cell to the center. This is a problem because you are aggregating data in a non-uniform distance. Take a look at the following figure for a visualization:

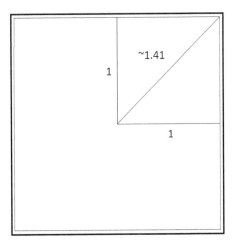

Figure 6.11: Square cell with distances from middle

Hex bins

While hex bins are quite new, they are starting to show up more frequently in maps. A hex bin map is very similar to a grid map as it is made up of equal cells that form a continuous surface, but a hex bin minimizes the varying distance from the center of the cell. This reduces the error in aggregating data, which makes the aggregation method more accurate. ArcGIS Pro has a tool that will easily create a hex bin surface on your map called **Generate Tessellation**. In the following exercise, you will learn how to create a hex bin map to aggregate the Uber pickups in Manhattan discussed earlier.

We will now see how to create a hex bin map. In this exercise, you will aggregate a large amount of Uber pickup data into hex bins to show the density of pickups around the island of Manhattan:

1. Open the `Chapter6.aprx` project and navigate to the **Uber Points Map** tab
2. Open the **Geoprocessing** pane by navigating to the **Analysis** tab and clicking on **Tools**
3. Search for **Generate Tessellation** and click on the tool
4. In **Output Feature Class** enter **EmptyHexBin**
5. Set **Extent** to the same layer as **Manhattan**
6. Set **Shape type** as **Hexagon**
7. Set the size to 250,000 square feet
8. Set **Spatial Reference** to **NAD 1983 StatePlane New York Long Island FIPS 3104 Feet**
9. Click on **Run**

This will generate a surface of hexagons that cover the entire island of Manhattan. You will notice that there are a lot of hexagons that are outside the island; we will take care of them in the following steps:

1. Click on the back button in the **Geoprocessing** pane until you get back to the **Search** bar
2. Search for **Summarize Within** and click on the tool
3. For **Input Polygons**, select **EmptyHexBin**
4. For **Input Summary Features**, select **UberPickupsManhattan201406**
5. For **Output Feature Class**, enter `PickupDensity`
6. Uncheck **Keep all input polygons** (this will remove the hexagons that contain no points)
7. Leave **Summary Fields** blank

8. Leave **Add shape summary attributes** checked
9. Leave **Group Field** blank
10. Click on **Run**

The **Summarize Within** tool will now count every point within each hexagon and write the count of points into a field of the **Output Feature Class**. You will need to symbolize the hex bins to show the count:

1. Click on the **PickupDensity** layer in your **Contents** pane
2. Move the **PickupDensity** layer to the top of your **Contents** pane so that it draws over the other layers
3. Click on the **Appearance** tab at the top of the window and click on **Symbology**
4. In the **Symbology**, pane change the drop-down under **Symbology** to **Graduated Colors**
5. Set **Field** to **Count of Points**
6. Leave **Normalization** as **<None>**
7. Set **Method** to **Quantile**
8. Set **Classes** to **5**
9. In the **Appearance Tab** at the top of the window, in the **Effects** area, set **Transparency** slider to **30%**

You now can see the streets show through the hex bins and see where there is a higher density of Uber pickups within Manhattan. This exercise showed you a simple way of creating a hex bin surface to aggregate large amounts of simple point data. If you were using points that had attributes, you can use the **Summarize Within** tool to give you statistical values of those attributes that you could symbolize.

Summary

In this chapter, you learned the common types of map that are created and when to choose and what type to use when creating your own map. Understanding the purpose of your map and the audience is key to making the best map for the job. You also learned how you can use cartographic license to generalize data to make your map clearer without taking away from the accuracy of your map and when it is okay to leave out labels. Understanding when you can take a hit in accuracy to make your map easier to understand will help create better maps. Finally, you learned how to properly aggregate data and what common methods you can employ to make large amounts of dense data easier to perceive.

In the next chapter, you will learn about coordinate systems, projections, how to take something that is 3D and put it on a 2D surface, and how important coordinate systems and projections are for keeping your data and analysis accurate.

7
Understanding and Choosing Projections

As mentioned previously in Chapter 1, *How Maps Get Made*, spatial data availability has skyrocketed in the past few years. Governments, non-profits, private companies, and individuals around the world are measuring and recording data, and tying that data to a location. The problem GIS professionals run into a lot is that all these different datasets have different ways of describing their location on Earth. If you have spent any time doing GIS, you may have run into issues when displaying data with different coordinate systems or projections. Working with projections is hard, and involves a lot of math. Luckily, ArcGIS Pro handles the math for you, but will do the wrong math if you tell it to. The software is very smart in converting projections, but is dumb, as it relies on the user to tell it what math to use. In this chapter, you will learn a brief background on how a location on Earth is more than a simple x, y coordinate. You will learn how location is derived, and how difficult it is to show a 3D surface on a 2D plane. You will learn the different ways you can project your data to fit the purpose of your map. Finally, you will learn how to properly choose a projection for your project.

In this chapter, we will cover the following topics:

- The world is round, and maps are flat
- Reconciling 3D to 2D
- Choosing a projection

The world is round, and maps are flat

Humans have known for a long time that the world is not flat. It is a spinning globe orbiting a star in outer space. In classrooms and homes around the world, people have world globes so they can reference or study them when they want to discuss location; however, there are two major problems with globes—scale and portability. For a globe to be physically practical, it must be able to fit through doorways and small enough for a person to maneuver. This, however, limits the amount of data that can be presented to the viewer. Globes are not very practical for travel space either, they are rigid and take up a lot of space. The simple solution for these problems is to use a flat map. A flat map can be folded or rolled for storage and transportation, and can be hung or laid out on a surface to be viewed. This is why almost all your interactions with maps are flat instead of round globes.

Taking that round globe and putting it on a flat surface is not easy, though. For example, say you have a large orange on a table, and it resembles Earth. You want to take this 3D object and make it flat, so you take your hand and start pressing down on the orange. Not only is juice going to start squirting out everywhere, but you'll also notice that the skin of the orange is starting to stretch and even tear. In GIS, we call this **distortion**. Distortion is when data has to be displaced to make it fit on a 2D plane. There is no way to prevent distortion, so as GIS professionals we have to make some choices to minimize the distortion we don't want, while allowing more distortion where we don't mind it.

The deceiving classroom map

All around the world, most children grew up looking at the **Mercator** world map. The Mercator projection, which is what is used in the Mercator map, was developed by Gerardus Mercator, a Flemish cartographer in the 16th century. His map was focused on preserving angular accuracy so that sailors could draw their headings in a straight line, and have that path be accurate throughout the length of the line. This projection helped sailors greatly by making it easier to navigate their ships around the known world. The problem in keeping the angular accuracy is that area and distance are not constant throughout the projection. The most well-known and obvious example of this inaccuracy is comparing *Greenland* and *Mexico*. Both of these countries have a very similar square area, but when you look at them on a Mercator world map, Greenland is much larger than Mexico. The reason for this is because the Mercator projection preserves the 90° angle of the intersections of longitude and latitude lines:

Figure 7.1: Mercator projection of the world

Reconciling 3D to 2D

The planet Earth may be round, but it is far from a perfect sphere. Because the Earth spins on an axis, centrifugal force actually bulges the center (equator) outwards. Gravity also plays a role as it is not constant across the entire Earth's surface, and many of the instruments that measure the Earth use gravity as a part of the measurement. These are some of the factors in geodesy. **Geodesy** is the science of accurately measuring and understanding Earth's geometric shape, orientation in space, and gravity field.

In the following two sections, you will get a brief overview of the pieces that make up your map projection. There is a lot of complicated math involved in these pieces, and to the regular GIS user there is little need to know the math; but if you find yourself doing more research work, it is highly recommended you research the math involved.

Geographic coordinate systems

To go from a 3D surface to a 2D plane, you first need to define the 3D surface. While there may be only one Earth, there are many ways of measuring it and classifying it. A **geographic coordinate system** is a 3D surface with a coordinate system to define location. You may be used to hearing locations in a geographic coordinate system as latitude and longitude. A geographic coordinate system is typically comprised of three elements—a geoid, a spheroid (or an ellipsoid), and a datum.

Geoid

Because of the rugged surface of the Earth and varying gravitational forces across it, geodesists developed a theoretical surface called the **geoid**. The geoid is the surface the Earth's oceans would take with no tides or currents. The surface of the water wouldn't be smooth because of the variations of gravity around the globe. This bumpy surface that is technically sea level at any point is what the geoid represents. The geoid represents a reference system for vertical measurement.

Spheroid

Because of the bumpy and irregular surface of the geoid, another surface was developed to help smooth the transition from 3D to 2D, and this is called a **spheroid**. A spheroid is a mathematical term for what is essentially a sphere that has been compressed or expanded in one axis. Geodesists create spheroids to closely match the geoid to a given extent. There are many spheroids in the world, and each one was created to handle different areas around the world, including spheroids for the whole of Earth. The spheroid represents a reference system for horizontal measurement.

Datum

Now that you have the geoid and spheroid, the last piece you need is a **datum**. A datum is what puts a coordinate grid on top of the spheroid. Much like spheroids, there are many datums that can be used. Some datums cover the whole world, like the **World Geodetic System 84** (**WGS 1984**), and some cover smaller areas like the **North American Datum 1983** (**NAD 1983**), which covers North America. Datums allow variation in topology versus a spheroid, because a spheroid is smooth and the surface of the Earth is not.

Transformations

Sometimes, you have multiple datasets, each with a different geographic coordinate system. While ArcGIS Pro can handle converting or transforming the data on the fly so the datasets show accurately, it requires a lot of processing power for larger datasets that could slow down your drawing performance considerably. It is usually recommended to transform your data into one geographic coordinate system so that you have only one reference to keep track of. Transforming from one geographic coordinate system to another can be tricky as there are many transformation methods available, and each one is specifically designed for specific transformations. For example, transforming from NAD 83 to WGS 84 has seven different methods:

- **NAD_1983_To_WGS_1984_1** covers the entire North American continent
- **NAD_1983_To_WGS_1984_2** covers the Alaskan Aleutian islands
- **NAD_1983_To_WGS_1984_3** covers Hawaii
- **NAD_1983_To_WGS_1984_5** covers the contiguous 48 states
- **NAD_1983_To_WGS_1984_6** covers the province of Quebec in Canada
- **NAD_1983_To_WGS_1984_7** covers the province of Saskatchewan in Canada
- **NAD_1983_To_WGS_1984_8** covers the province of Alberta in Canada

So, just like choosing your geographic coordinate system is based on the location of your data, so is your transformation. You may notice that the transformations listed earlier by their name, imply that the transformation goes from NAD 1983 to WGS 1984, but this is not the case. Transformations can be used in both directions, so you can transform WGS 1984 to NAD 1983 using the listed projections as well.

Projected coordinate systems

In the previous section, we discussed how to put a coordinate system onto a 3D surface, but we still have to take that surface and project it onto a 2D plane. To do this, you need to choose a projected coordinate system or projection. An easy way of imaging how you take a geographic coordinate system and put it into a projection is to imagine the geographic coordinate system as a desktop globe with the latitude and longitude lines painted onto it. Imagine putting a light in the middle of the globe so that the latitude and longitude lines project out. You can hold out a piece of flat paper close to the globe, and see the lines projected onto it. This is a simplified example of how projections work. You can bend and contort the paper to make it project the way you want. You can also have the piece of paper cut through the globe. Any place that the paper touches the globe is where you have zero error. The further the paper is from the surface of the globe, the more error is introduced. Further, you will see the three most common ways the 2D plane can contort to follow the spheroid.

Cylindrical

Imagine you took the piece of paper you had before and made it into a cylinder, and was able to wrap all the way around the globe where the paper and globe touched the paper a full 360°. Once the coordinate system is projected onto the cylinder, you cut it opposite of where you want the center of your projection to be. The center of your projection is called the **central meridian**. The orientation of the globe to the cylinder is important, and can be categorized in three ways:

- **Normal aspect**: When the cylinder touches the globe along a latitude line like the equator
- **Transverse aspect**: When the cylinder touches the globe along a longitude line like the prime meridian
- **Oblique aspect**: When the cylinder touches the globe along an arbitrary line determined by the creator of the projection

The **cylindrical** projection is the basis of the Mercator map we discussed earlier in *The deceiving classroom map* section. The following is an example of the normal cylindrical projection used in the Mercator map:

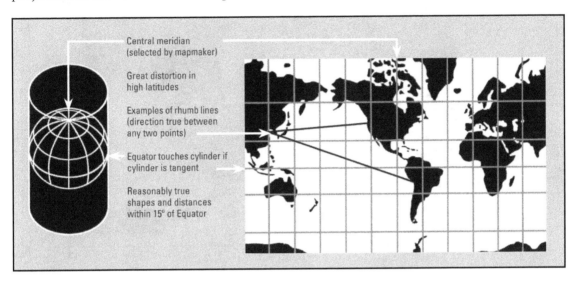

Figure 7.2: Cylindrical projection. Source: USGS

Conic

Again, imagine the piece of paper as a cone, much like a party hat, and you have the basis of the **conic** projection. You can place the cone on top of the globe, and once the coordinate system is projected onto it, cut opposite the central meridian and lay it out flat.

The following is an example of the conic projection with the **Lambert Conformal Conic (LCC)** projection:

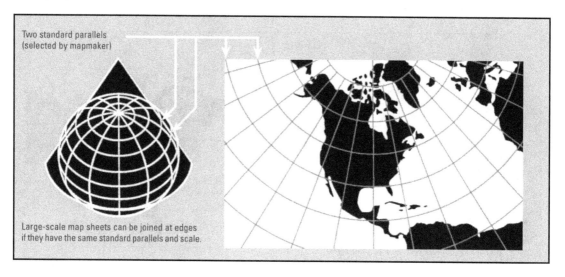

Figure 7.3: Conic projection. Source: USGS

Planar

Now, imagine we have the paper flat again, and the middle of the paper touches the globe. We are using an undistorted plane to project the coordinate system onto. As you can imagine, the outside edges of the paper are far away from the globe, so your accuracy is high where the paper touches the globe, but gets more inaccurate as you move away from the center. Much like the cylinder projection, a **planar** projection can be categorized in three ways:

- **Equatorial aspect**: When the plane touches the equator
- **Polar aspect**: When the plane touches the North or South Poles
- **Oblique aspect**: When the plane touches an arbitrary line determined by the creator of the projection

Consider the following figure to get a brief of different planar projection:

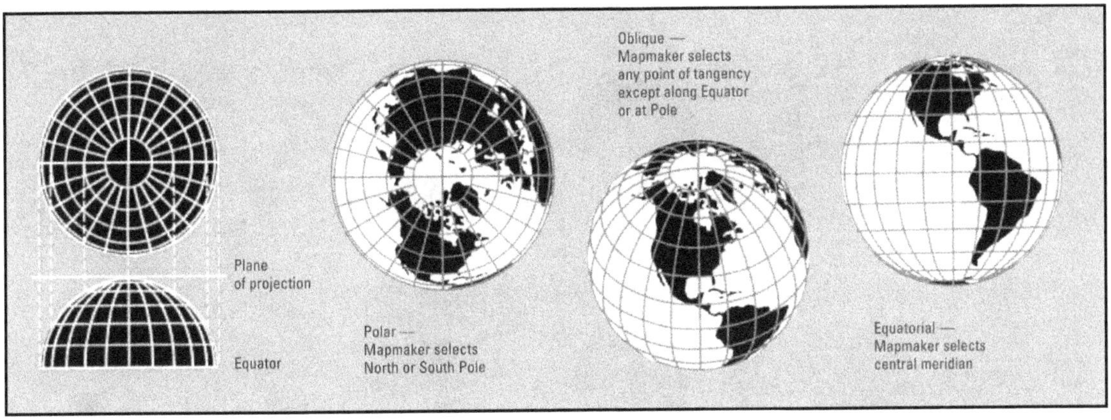

Figure 7.4: Planar aspect diagram. Source: USGS

Unlike the cylindrical and conic projections, planar has one more attribute to describe it—perspective. In cylindrical and conic projections, the perspective is typically the center of the spheroid, and projects perpendicularly out from it. For planar, there are four perspectives that can be used:

- **Gnomonic**: When the perspective is in the center of the spheroid.
- **Stereographic**: When the perspective is on the opposite side of the spheroid of where the plane touches.
- **Orthographic**: When the perspective is infinity. You can imagine this as what the spheroid would look like from the perspective of the plane, much like an image from a satellite.
- **Azimuthal**: When the perspective is tangent on the plane to any point on the spheroid.

The following are examples of the four planar projection perspectives:

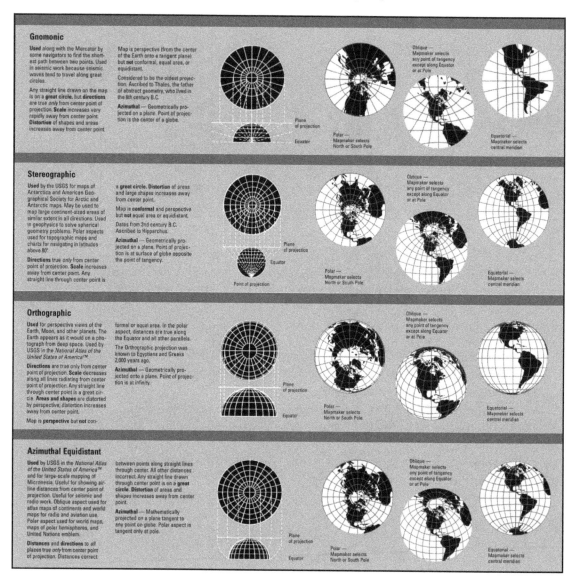

Figure 7.5: Planar projections. Source: USGS

There is a fourth, not so common plane, called **Pseudocylindric**. It is a different take on the cylindrical projection. It can be seen in the Robinson style map of the world.

Now that you know the common types of projections, you need to know that there is a common occurrence with projections—you can have the projection cut through the spheroid, giving you more than one point of contact. When the plane crosses through the spheroid, it's called being **secant**. In the examples mentioned earlier, all the projections were tangent, which means they never cut through the spheroid. You would choose a secant projection to reduce area distortion.

There are thousands of projections already inside ArcGIS Pro, so you don't have to worry about adding them. ArcGIS Pro will, in most cases, automatically detect the projection being used and apply it and transform it on the fly to another if you are working in another projection. You can also create your own projection system and add it into ArcGIS Pro. Be mindful if you are editing data in different coordinate systems, as this could lead to inaccurate data.

Distortion

No matter the final projection you use, you will have to live with distortion in your map. Depending on the type of map you are creating, you will typically want to preserve one of three things—angle, area, and distance. A projection name will typically tell you what it is preserving by using the following nomenclature:

- **Conformal**: Preserves angle and shape within the map
- **Equal-area**: Preserves the area within the map
- **Equidistant**: Preserves distance within the map

For example, the projection system, **NAD 1983 State Plane California II FIPS 0402 Feet**, uses the Lambert Conformal Conic projection. This tells you that the projection preserves angle and shape using a conical projection plane. Lambert was derived from a projection created by Johann Heinrich Lambert in the 18th century.

Going back to the earlier example of the Mercator projection (*Figure 7.1*), we know that the map was designed so sailors were able to draw straight lines for headings that would stay accurate throughout the map. This means it is a conformal map, as it preserves angle and shape. Looking back to Greenland on the Mercator map, the shape of the land mass is accurate, it's just that it is too large in relation to other parts of the map. Also, distance varies between two points as you move away from the equator. This map is great for sailors; however, it is not so great at showing the true size of the land masses on Earth.

A good way of visualizing the distortion of a projection is to use what are called **Tissot's indicatrices**. These are circles of equal area placed in a grid on a map to show the distortion of a specific area of a map. The following is a map using the WGS 1984 Web Mercator (Auxiliary Sphere) projection. This is the standard projection for web mapping. You can see how the circles start to get more and more distorted as you move north or south of the equator. This shows that the map is most accurate around the equator; if you were creating a map for Canada or Russia, you would probably not want to use this projection:

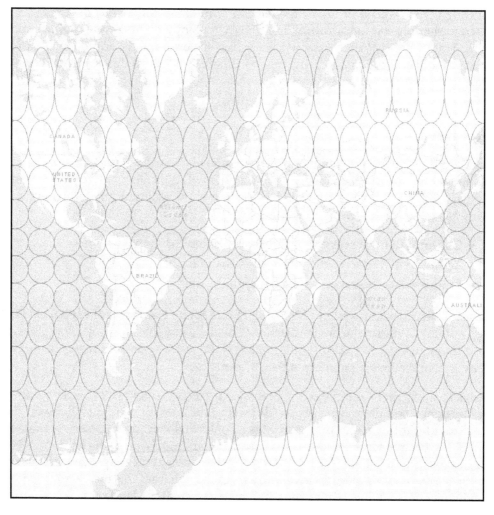

Figure 7.6: Tissot's circles on a Mercator projection of the world

State plane coordinate systems

In the previous section, you saw a projection called NAD 1983 State Plane California II FIPS 0402. If you have spent any time around a land surveyor in the United States, you must have heard the term **state plane** a lot. The state plane coordinate system is not a single projection, but a collection of projections for the United States. Each state has at least one state plane projection. For states that have more than one projection, they classify each as a zone, and the zones do not overlap. As we can see in the preceding figure, the projection is of Zone 2 of California, and California has a total of six zones using the NAD 1983 geographic coordinate system. In the older NAD 1927 geographic coordinate system, California had seven. The following is a map of the current state plane zones in the United States using NAD 1983:

Figure 7.7: State plane zones of the United States

You might notice something a little peculiar—some states have their zones east/west, and some have theirs north/south. This was a decision by each state based on the recommendations of land surveyors and the regulatory bodies each state has. Not every state uses the same type of projection. These state plane coordinate systems are favored by land surveyors, because they break the surface of the Earth up into relatively small areas that produce an error rate of no more than 1:100,00.Cities and municipalities typically use the state plane zone that they are located in for their data for two reasons—the low error introduced, and because it's an accepted and well-known standard that makes it easy for an outsider to guess with high certainty what projection will be used. One other feature of the state plane coordinate system is there are no negative coordinates. The origin, or (0,0) of each zone is outside the zone, meaning all coordinates will be positive, which makes calculations easier and less prone to error.

Choosing a projection

Now that you've had a quick overview of some of the more common geographic and projection coordinate systems, you should have some understanding of how your projection choice can change the look of your map. But of all the thousands of choices of projections that ArcGIS Pro gives you, which one should you use? This is dependent on the scale and shape of your data, and what the purpose of your map is. It is usually best to choose the smallest projection that all your data fits into. This will minimize the distortion that can be introduced when using larger projections. For example, if you are mapping world capitals, you wouldn't want to use a continent or country-based projection, you would want to use a world projection. On the other hand, if you are mapping clean water locations in Libya, you wouldn't want to use a projection based on the North American Datum.

Scale of your data

It is important to understand the full spatial extent of your data. The size, shape, and location of your data plus the purpose of your map, will drive what projection to use. Here are some questions you should ask before choosing a projection:

- What area does the data cover?
- What is the shape of the data?
- What aspect do I want to preserve?

You want to first understand where your data will lay on your map. This will help you narrow down which projections to use, like choosing a planet, continent, country, or smaller projection. Also, you must be mindful of what shape the data is. The common projections you have learned about so far are planar, cylindrical, and conic. Respectively, these are round, rectangular, and triangular shapes. Looking at the full extent of your data, a general shape can be drawn around it. If your data is mostly in the shape of a circle, you would typically want to choose a planar projection. If your data is more linear or rectangular, you would typically choose a cylindrical projection; and if your data is more triangular in shape, you would typically choose a conic projection. Once you have answered these questions, you should be able to narrow down your choice of projection.

Coordinate system properties

In ArcGIS Pro, you can view the coordinate systems in an easy-to-use **Coordinate System** properties section in the map **Properties** window. This **Properties** window is also available when you create a **New Feature Class** or raster. The following will run through an exercise where you will change the projection of an existing **Map Frame**:

1. Open `Chapter7.aprx`, and you should see a **Map Frame** called **Choosing a projection**. Click it to bring it up, if it's not already. You can see that there is a layer called **Contiguous 48**, which is the contiguous 48 states of the USA.

2. In the **Contents** pane, right-click **Choosing a projection** and select **Properties**, then click **Coordinate System** on the left. This will bring up the **Coordinate System** properties window:

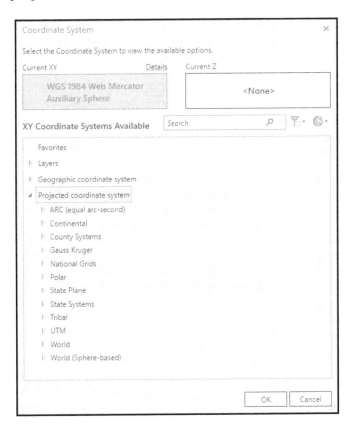

Figure 7.8: Coordinate system window

At the top, you have two boxes that show the **Current XY** coordinate system and the **Current Z** coordinate system. The **Current XY** will have the current projection of the map that is currently selected. Following that, there is a larger box with the heading **XY Coordinate Systems Available**. This is where you can browse the different coordinate systems available to you. They are in four categories: **Favorites**, **Layers**, **Geographic coordinate system**, and **Projected coordinate system**. You can also see a **Search** bar and two icons above the box—the **Spatial Filter** and the **Add Coordinate System**. Notice that the **Current XY** box is highlighted blue. This indicates that you are currently selecting an XY coordinate system. To select a Z coordinate system, click the box following **Current Z**.

The **Spatial Filter** button is a great new feature for ArcGIS Pro. This button will allow you to filter out coordinate systems that your data falls into, so you don't have to scroll through thousands of projections. When you click the **Spatial Filter** button, you get two options—**Set Spatial Filter** and **Clear Spatial Filter**. Click **Set Spatial Filter** if you want to set a filter, and click **Clear Spatial Filter** to reset the list of coordinate systems. The following is the window that appears when you click **Set Spatial Filter**:

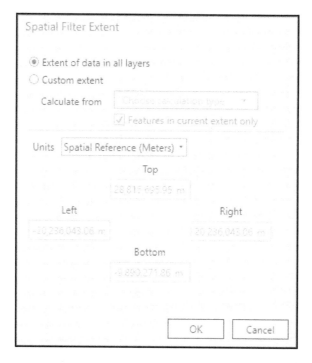

Figure 7.9: Spatial filter window

You have two choices—**Extent of data in all layers**, and **Custom extent**. **Extent of data in all layers** will take the extent of every piece of data you have in your map, and filter projections that cover all the layers in your map. **Custom extent** gives you a few options in choosing your filter; you can choose the current visible extent of your map, or choose a specific layer in your map ignoring the rest of the layers. Choosing visible extent will show projections that cover just the area visible in your **Map Frame**. Choosing a specific layer is useful if you have, for example, a worldwide basemap in your map and don't want to see coordinate systems for areas outside your map area. The following this is where you make this selection are extent boxes. Here, you can enter in your own **Custom extent** to filter coordinate systems. These boxes will automatically be populated with the extent of the visible extent or layer you choose. You can also change the units of the extent with the drop-down box next to **Units**.

Looking back to the **XY Coordinate Systems Available** box in the **Coordinate System** window, there are four categories of coordinate systems. The following is the description of each category for the XY coordinate system:

- **Favorites**: Contains either geographic or projected coordinate systems that you want to keep on hand to quickly choose. You can add a coordinate system to **Favorites** by clicking the **Coordinate System**, and then clicking the small box with a yellow star and a plus sign to the right of your selection.
- **Layers**: Contains the coordinate systems of layers that are already in your map. This makes it easy to make sure you are choosing a coordinate system already being used in your map.
- **Geographic coordinate system**: A list of geographic coordinate systems.
- **Projected coordinate system**: A list of projected coordinate systems.

Each of these categories are collapsed lists; click the small triangle to the left of each to expand the list. Expand the **Projected coordinate system** category. You can see there are more categories to choose from, and they are categorized by location or type. Take some time to search through the different categories to see all the options available to you.

You want to choose a projection that works for the contiguous 48 states. To make your choice easier, you can filter the coordinate systems using the layer:

1. Click the **Spatial Filter** button next to the **Search** bar and click **Set Spatial Filter**.
2. Select **Custom Extent**, and in the drop-down next to **Calculate from**, select **Contiguous 48** then click **OK**.
3. While there doesn't seem to be much change, expand the **National Grids** category and you'll notice that there are only projections for **Canada**, **North America**, and **Oceans**. Your filter worked.

4. Now you want to find the **North America Albers Equal Area Conic** projection. This can be found in **Continental | North America**, or you can search for it in the **Search** bar. Select it.

Next, we want to look at the details of the projection you just chose. To do this, click **Details** on the top-right of the **Current XY** box. This will bring up the **Coordinate System Details** window as follows:

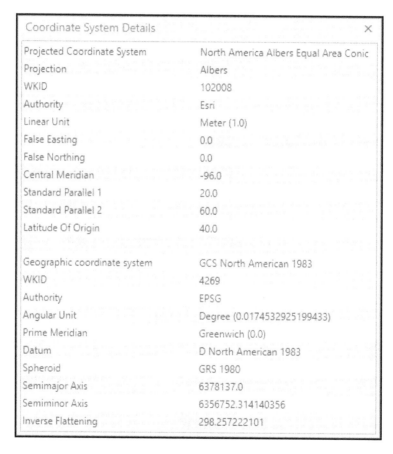

Coordinate System Details	×
Projected Coordinate System	North America Albers Equal Area Conic
Projection	Albers
WKID	102008
Authority	Esri
Linear Unit	Meter (1.0)
False Easting	0.0
False Northing	0.0
Central Meridian	-96.0
Standard Parallel 1	20.0
Standard Parallel 2	60.0
Latitude Of Origin	40.0
Geographic coordinate system	GCS North American 1983
WKID	4269
Authority	EPSG
Angular Unit	Degree (0.0174532925199433)
Prime Meridian	Greenwich (0.0)
Datum	D North American 1983
Spheroid	GRS 1980
Semimajor Axis	6378137.0
Semiminor Axis	6356752.314140356
Inverse Flattening	298.257222101

Figure 7.10: Coordinate system details window

There is a lot of information about the projection in this window, and while seeing it all is great, most of the time you will not need it. Let's focus on a few important details in this window:

- **Projection**: The type of projection method used.
- **WKID**: Stands for **Well-Known ID**. This is a unique code given to projections and geographic coordinate systems. You can actually search for projections in ArcGIS Pro using this number.
- **Authority**: The governing body of the WKID. In this window, there are two WKIDs: one for the projected coordinate system, and one for the geographic coordinate system. You can see there are two different authorities: **Esri** and **European Petroleum Survey Group** (**EPSG**). EPSG was the first group to give codes to coordinate systems.
- **Linear Unit**: The unit of measurement of the coordinates in the projection.
- **Standard Parallel:** Where the projection touches or cuts through the spheroid, and where your most accurate area of the projection is.

Close this window and then click **OK**. You'll notice that the northern boundary of the US is now curved instead of straight using the WGS 1984 Web Mercator projection. As the name implies, this projection preserves an area and uses a conic projection. This projection is widely used by the USGS, as it is best used for wide and short data in the mid-latitudes, like the contiguous 48.

Let's look at a projection that isn't designed for your data to see what happens. You are going to change the coordinate system to **NAD 1983 UTM Zone 10N**. This can be found by searching for it or finding it under **Projected Coordinate System|UTM|NAD 1983**. **Universal Transverse Mercator** (**UTM**) is a worldwide system. It breaks the world into zones along lines of longitude, so it looks like long vertical strips of the world. Zone 10, which we are using, is the zone that covers the western half of California. When you project your map with it, you'll notice that most of the east coast is now missing. The map just ends. You'll also notice that the contiguous 48 are now tilted, so California is level to the latitudes. This is because Zone 10 is only supposed to cover a small geographic area. The rest of the world would be too distorted to visualize meaningfully. It is an example like this that shows how choosing the right projection is very important.

Elevation or the Z

One of the most exciting features of ArcGIS Pro is the ability to natively show 3D data, and just like 2D data there are spatial references for defining elevation. For Z values, there are a lot less choices in coordinate systems; however, choosing the correct coordinate system is very important. An incorrect vertical coordinate system can cause many problems in accuracy, even horizontally. For example, if you mix up the vertical coordinate system of a building, your shade analysis could be off by dozens or hundreds of feet horizontally!

Vertical coordinate systems

Many devices now have GPS units in them, which means you can take measurements out in the field even easier; however, just like how you have to take a horizontal geographic coordinate system and project it, you must do something similar for vertical measurements. When using a GPS unit, you can get an elevation for a location and this elevation is based on a spheroid model, specifically the WGS 84 reference spheroid. The spheroid model is not related to sea level, and height above sea level is how most elevations are given in the real world. The height above sea level is called the **geoid height**. To get the geoid height, you must project the elevation. There are many tools that can perform this for you, but it can get complicated really quickly. ArcGIS Pro can project vertical elevation to a height above sea level after you choose the proper datum. For example, the current vertical datum for North America is the **North American Vertical Datum 1988** (**NAVD 88**). NAVD 88 superseded the **National Geodetic Vertical Datum 1929** (**NGVD 29**), which a lot of legacy elevation data referenced. There is typically, around a 3.6-foot difference between the two datums, so be sure you are using the correct datum!

Tidal datums

Not all data is above sea level - GIS handles data underwater or deep within the Earth. When working with maritime maps you'll see terms like **Mean Lower Low Water** (**MLLW**) or **Mean High Water** (**MHW**), which are variations of the elevation of sea level. As you may already know, the oceans and even larger bodies of water have tides, which means sea level is constantly in flux. These terms reference the elevation of water during specific average tidal states. There are thousands of tidal stations along the coasts around the world taking real-time measurements of the tidal height to feed into tidal datums. In the United States, **National Oceanic and Atmospheric Administration** (**NOAA**) uses the past 19 years' worth of data to create the tidal datum.

The following are the most common variations of tidal datums:

- **Mean Lower Low Water** (**MLLW**): The average of the lower low water height of each tidal day observed over the **National Tidal Datum Epoch** (**NTDE**)
- **Mean Low Water** (**MLW**): The average of all the low water heights of each tidal day observed over the NTDE
- **Mean High Water** (**MHW**): The average of all the high water heights of each tidal day observed over the NTDE
- **Mean Higher High Water** (**MHHW**): The average of the higher high water height of each tidal day observed over the NTDE

One of the reasons to have these variations in tidal datums is to allow sailors to make informed decisions on where they go in the shallower water. For example, a lot of maritime charts will show the Mean Lower Low Water, because it will show the shallowest depths an area will have. So, a sailor will know that even in the lowest tide, they can chart a safe course in shallow water and not run aground. For coastal projects where sea intrusion is a concern, you would use the Mean Higher High Water elevation, as that is the highest average elevation of sea level that will appear.

Summary

In this chapter, you learned a lot about geographic coordinate systems, projected coordinate systems, and the pieces that make up these systems. You learned the basic principles of choosing a projection for your data and map. While it may not have felt like it, this chapter only scratched the surface of coordinate systems. Understanding and correctly applying geographic coordinate systems and projected coordinate systems will set you apart from novice GIS users. Coordinate systems are probably the most important portion of GIS, because no matter how good your map or analysis looks, if the spatial data used in that analysis has the wrong geographic coordinate system or projected coordinate system, then your data is wrong. Having the wrong projection can cost a project a lot of time and money when the real world doesn't match up with the data and map you created.

In the next chapter, you will learn ways of decluttering your map and producing clean and visually appealing symbology, so that viewers of your map aren't confused or distracted from the true purpose of your map. For further information, you may refer to: `https://oceanservice.noaa.gov/facts/geodesy.html`.

8
Clean Symbology and Uncluttered Maps

From an early age, we are trained to attach meaning to symbols, and the use of symbols on maps is one of the first things novice map readers identify as a key component of maps. All symbols are an abstraction of reality, but can range from highly realistic to highly abstract, while others are essentially an extension of the alphabet. Some symbols are universally recognizable to large groups, others to only a few people. The whole map is essentially a symbol, and at the same time, an assemblage of symbols.

In this chapter, we will cover the following topics:

- Representing features with graphics
- Classifying data
- Making symbols dynamic

Representing features with graphics

Graphic marks are considered to be symbols when they are agreed to have a certain meaning. This could be a picnic table to identify a park site, or a blue cross to identify a hospital. Others are more specific to maps—the use of a circle to represent a city, for example. The mapmaker assigns a symbol that represents the information he or she wants to bring across to the map user. Good, intuitive symbols can often be presented without defining them in a legend, but for most purposes, we add a legend to ensure clarity.

Symbol systems and symbol conventions

Many organizations that produce volumes of maps have rigid symbol systems that are the same on every map they produce. The topographic maps of the **United States Geological Survey** (**USGS**) have a multiple-page booklet for all of their symbols, and every major travel map company has their own version of the expected roadside symbols. If we are familiar with an area, we may attach memories and personal meaning to those symbols, and those memories affect how we interpret new areas when we see those same symbols.

Apart from the continuity of a single mapping organization, there are conventions we carry to any map reading from our experiences—a band of red outlined in thin black is almost always going to be a road, and a circle with a label next to it is most likely a city name. Like learning the alphabet, this training helps us read a map we've never seen before. As mapmakers, it's our responsibility to work with this understanding. If we create new symbols for a feature set, we cannot move so far beyond our reader's training that they are unable to comprehend the map. Even with a legend, if we represent coffee shops with an elephant, the reader has to constantly refer to the legend, because the cognitive dissonance is too great.

Symbols are classified according to the degree to which they look like the things they represent. **Realistic symbols** (also called **mimetic**, **pictorial**, or **replicative**) look like what they represent. For example, an orchard might be represented with rows of tiny trees. These types of symbols can be easy to interpret and are unambiguous, which makes them easier to read without a legend; however, it can be difficult to design an entire symbol set, and they may start to look similar if there are too many feature types represented.

The converse of realistic symbols are **abstract symbols**, which often take the form of a geometric shape (and may sometimes be called **geometric symbols**). These don't look like what they represent, so may be harder to interpret without a legend, but may be easier to remember and design. Patterns in the data may also stand out more clearly across a map, as they are generally less detailed. We can also use text as abstraction, although these symbols are less common in maps for international audiences due to their language-specific context. But if language is not a barrier, we might easily indicate a hospital with an **H**, or a parking lot with a **P**, as seen in the following image:

Figure 8.1: Symbols made from text

Icons and pictographs may or may not have any direct connection to what they identify. They may be representational, such as an airplane to designate airports, or stylized trees to symbolize a forest. In hazard mapping, risks, such as flooding or blizzard conditions, may be represented with waves or a snowflake symbol. Others may be representative of an organizational logo, or stylized graphic. The major problem associated with symbology is that we have no standards. Everyone designs their own, or uses the symbols designed in a software package. Sometimes, symbols are carried over from older software that have little meaning to newer users. A floppy disk icon is a relatively universal icon for saving one's work, but when was the last time you used one? As a result, we see many different symbols to represent the same things. Cultural differences can also result in different interpretations of intuitive symbology; for example, the Red Cross, which is represented logically enough by a big red cross, is known as the Red Crescent in Islamic countries, and as such is represented by a crescent shape instead of a cross. It's important to select symbols that are appropriate to the theme of the map, and will clearly reveal the pattern of data.

Scales of measurement

In addition to identifying data as purely qualitative or quantitative, we also need to understand the level or scale of measurement used to collect the data which, at times, is also known as **data types**. **Scales of measurement** refer to the method by which we can organize and classify data. The four scales are nominal, ordinal, interval, and ratio, and each have different properties that must be considered when symbolizing them:

- **Nominal data**: This can be categorized, such as animal, mineral or vegetable, objects, with the same value of some attribute. The values have no standard numeric value, meaning that no mathematical operations can be performed, even if the value looks like a number. For example, postal zip codes may be composed entirely of numbers, but they are really just labels, because we don't add or multiply them. They also cannot be ordered in any meaningful way. You might be able to sort them alphabetically, but that's not really meaningful in terms of symbolization. We can't use a symbol set that implies quantitative differences, because there aren't any.
- **Ordinal data**: It can be ranked, but the intervals are indeterminate. Satisfaction surveys are a great example of this. My estimation of 4-star service might be different than yours, and there's no clear way to tell if the difference between 3.5 and 4 is the same as 4 to 4.5. So, while we have an idea of more, we can't properly quantify it, which means any statistical analysis is limited, and subject to flawed assumptions. In this case, we can use symbols that imply quantity, but it's important to understand the limitations.

- **Interval data**: It moves us into the realm of mathematical calculations, but just barely. The intervals are all the same size, but there is no meaningful zero. A common example of this is temperature data, where 0°C is just another value on the scale, rather than an absence of temperature. With interval data, we know that each interval on the scale is the same size. For example, the difference between 12 and 13 is the same as the difference between 67 and 68; however, since zero is just another value, we can't look at the thermometer and say that 80°C is twice as hot as 40°C. Instead, we might use a combination of qualitative and quantitative symbology here, or combine two quantitative methods, such as color and value.

- **Ratio data**: It has both meaningful intervals and a real zero, which means that all quantitative options are open to us. The intervals are the same size at any point in the scale, and the ratios also work—an increase of 5 means the same at any value, and 40 is half of 80. Ratio data should always be represented with some sort of quantitative scheme, as the numeric values are the key aspect of the data being displayed.

If you've never thought about data this way before, it can be a little confusing. The flowchart in the following figure can help you decide:

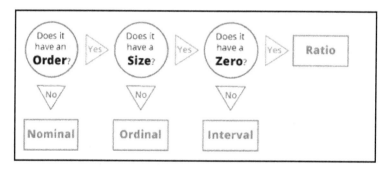

Figure 8.2: Determining scales of measurement

Visual variables

The design of symbols requires attention to their visual dimensions. According to Jacques Bertin (1967), the ways in which we can vary a symbol's quality are:

- Shape
- Size
- Orientation

- Hue (color)
- Value
- Texture

Some of these are easier to interpret than others. The cartographic designer makes selections on the basis of visual dimensions, and the symbol's functionality is tied to the level (or scale) of measurement of the data.

Size, value, and texture can convey quantitative differences. Shape and orientation are exclusively qualitative, and color hue (not value) tends to be qualitative as well, unless used as part of a diverging scheme (as seen previously in `Chapter 5`, *Picking Colors with Confidence*). For example, we can draw circles sized proportionally to values in a dataset, where the size variations correspond to intervals in the array. Size, however, cannot be the visual dimension when we scale symbols to nominal data, because we do not know the numerical distance between nominal classes. Also, if our map needs to be produced in black and white, color is not an available dimension.

We may also use redundant coding and combine two qualities, such as **Size** and **Value**, to reinforce our message. This needs to be done carefully to avoid misleading our audience, but can be very effective when used well:

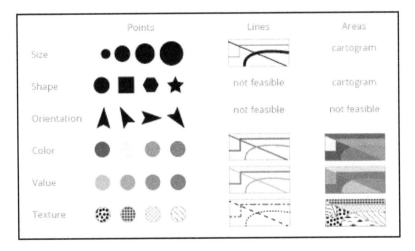

Figure 8.3: Visual variables. (Bertin, 1967)

Thematic maps can be either qualitative or quantitative, which impacts the way in which we represent the data. The chief purpose of qualitative mapping is to show the locational characteristics of phenomena or data. Amounts, other than the observation possible by comparing map areas, are not the content communicated by qualitative mapping. Quantitative maps, by contrast, are expressly designed to demonstrate numeric information, and map colors and symbol types must reflect that information appropriately.

The dimensional qualities of each symbol type (point, line, and area) have a unique graphic expression for each map type. There is a traditional correlation between geographical phenomena (point, line, area, and volume) and the employment of symbol types. Point data (for example, cities at the appropriate scale) is customarily mapped by point symbols, such as dots or scaled circles. Roads, which are linear phenomena, can be mapped by line symbols. Geographical phenomena, having an areal extent (lakes, countries, or nations), can be mapped with patterns or tints that fill the area. However, the match is not always convenient.

We also sometimes use lines to represent non-linear features, such as with **isolines**. Elevation represented with contour lines is a great example of an area feature represented by lines. Other types of isolines include bathymetry, **isogones** (magnetic declination), **isochrones** (time), and many more. The three symbol types (point, line, and area) may be matched to the measurement scales to produce a valuable typology of map symbols. We'll take a look at using and customizing each of these in ArcPro.

Point symbols

Point symbols can be used to represent actual point features, something that occurs at a single location, or as a proxy for an area feature. The scale of the map plays a large role in defining what counts as a single location, but can also determine whether or not an area feature is represented as a point. The most obvious example of the latter is probably cities. Depending on the scale and purpose of your map, you might choose to represent the actual urban expanse, or you might represent different sized cities with different sized circles, as we saw in our example in `Chapter 4`, *Typographic Principles*.

In our example, we'll practice with schools, which are almost always represented as point features, except in detailed building footprint maps:

1. Open the **Chapter 8** project, `ch8.aprx`. The data in this project has been downloaded from the *City of Sacramento GIS* (`http://data.cityofsacramento.org/`), and you can search and download additional layers for practice.

2. Click the **public schools** symbol in the **Contents** pane to open the **Symbology** pane.

3. In the search box, type `school`, and set the drop-down to **All styles**. Press the *Enter* key.

4. Ignore the 3D symbols, these never look good on 2D maps. You should see several options for symbols below the 3D options. Select school from **Icon Points**.

5. Change the size to **12 pt**, and click **Apply**.
This works well enough, but let's say we want to use something a little less boxy. ArcPro lets you bring in your own images, either that you've created, or that you've downloaded. Make sure you read the restrictions for use on any downloaded imagery; some may be free for personal use, but require purchase for commercial applications. Proceed with the following steps.

6. Click the **Layers** button on the **Symbology** pane. Under **Insert shape**, click **File** and **Browse** to the `Ch8 images` folder.

7. Select `school.svg`, and click **Open**. Most of the options to set properties for the **Symbol** are missing, but don't worry, we can still customize our icon.

8. Click the **Symbol** button, and set the **Color** to Tuscan Red, and the size to **20 pt**. Click **Apply**.

9. Return to the **Layers** settings, and notice that the options have returned. You can now set outline colors and widths, and change the fill properties from solid to gradient, although these options are best used for simple symbols rather than something as complex as our schoolhouse. You can also use the **Shape marker** options to use symbols from fonts, such as Wingdings, or our hospital or parking examples prior.

10. Turn on the major hospitals layer (**maj_hosp**), and click the symbol in the **Contents** pane.

11. This time, in the **Layers** settings, under **Insert shape**, select **Font**.

12. There is a **hospital** symbol in the **Esri Default Marker** font, but we are going to make our own. Change the font to **Calibri** (or a similar Sans-serif font).

13. Set the font style to **Bold**, and select the capital **H**. Click **OK**.

14. Change the **Shape fill** symbol to **Solid fill** with outline (**0.5 pt**), and set the **Color** to White and the outline to Black.

15. Change the size to **16 pt**.

16. Click the **Structure** button (small wrench), and under **Layers**, click the **Add symbol layer**.

17. Select **Marker layer** (a circle will appear), and then drag this new layer underneath the **H** layer using the three small dots at the left of the symbol (as shown in the following figure):

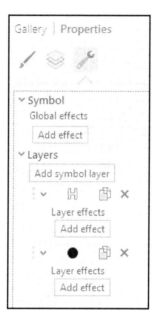

Figure 8.4: Adding a symbol layer

18. Switch back to **Layers**, and highlight your new (circle) layer.
19. Under **Appearance**, click the **Shapes** button and select the rounded rectangle.
20. Change the **Shape fill** symbol to solid fill (no outline), and set the **Color** to Blue and click **Apply**. The outline shape is probably a little tight on the **H**, so we can either shrink the letter, or enlarge the box. Let's do a little of both.
21. Change the rectangle size to **12 pt**, and click **Apply**. This makes a nice sized symbol to go along with our schools.
22. Highlight the **H** layer at the top, then set the size to **14 pt** and click **Apply**.
23. Now that the **H** is smaller, the outline is interfering with readability, so set the outline to **0 pt**. You should have a nice, clean white **H** on a blue field that is easy to spot on your map.

Now we have two symbols that are pretty easily identified and are distinct from each other, so that a pattern can quickly be seen. Let's save those to our styles so we can use them in other projects:

1. Create a new style for this chapter—on the **Insert** tab, select **New | New Style**. Name it Ch8, and click **OK**.
2. Select the **hospital** symbol in the **Contents** pane.
3. Click the **Menu** button in the upper-right corner of the **Symbology** panel and select **Save symbol to style**.
4. Give it a name that will help you identify it later, and click **OK**. You can also use **Category** and **Tags** to organize your symbols.
5. By default, this will save in the **Favorites** style, but use the drop-down to select your **Chapter 8** style (Ch8.stylx).
6. Repeat for the **schoolhouse** symbol:

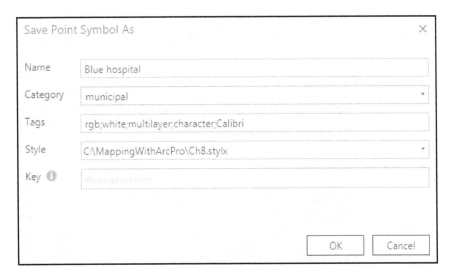

Figure 8.5: Saving your hard work to a style

To use these symbols in another project, instead of recreating the symbol, or browsing through your files for them, you can select them from the **Gallery**. If the styles you want aren't visible in the **Gallery**, select **Add** from the **Insert** tab.

Want to use your styles from ArcMap? Use **Insert | Import** to convert your old .style files to .stylx. Don't worry, your old styles will still be there for use in ArcMap, as this process creates a copy for conversion.

Line symbols

With **line symbols,** we can also move beyond defaults. Lines can have casings (outlines), and variable dash lengths, to add information and create a hierarchy where appropriate. Let's work on the light rail symbol:

1. Select the light rail symbol in the **Contents** pane.
2. In the gallery, search for rail. You should see a couple of results with the traditional railroad symbol of a line with cross hatches. These can be difficult to work with, as the hatching makes the symbol noisier, and sometimes in tight quarters, the angles get a little strange. This symbol is also typically reserved for heavy rail.
3. Select the gray and white symbol from **Scheme 3** (hover over the symbol to see the details).
4. Switch to **Properties | Layers**, and notice how this symbol is constructed—a solid, dark gray line, and a dashed, light gray line on top. The colors for the rail system are blue and yellow, so it might be helpful to use these colors on the map, to help form a mental connection with the trains.
5. Set the bottom line to Pacific Blue, and the top (dashed) line to Medium Yellow. Click **Apply**.
6. Switch the colors, and notice how that changes the overall appearance of the line, even though it appears to be made of evenly spaced dashes. If we look at the **Dash effect** (as seen in the following figure), we can see that, in fact, they aren't quite evenly spaced; the **Dash template** reads 6 7, which means a 6 pt line followed by a 7 pt space. Feel free to play with these settings and observe the effects:

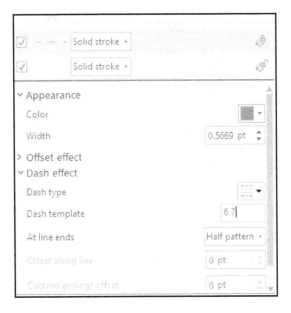

Figure 8.6: Dash effect settings

7. Turn on the **bikemasterplan** layer.
8. For this layer, we want to differentiate between existing and proposed paths, so we'll select **Unique Values**, and set the **Field** to **EX_PROP**.
9. We don't need to show any other values besides existing and proposed, so click **More**, and uncheck **Show all other values**.
10. Click the symbol for **Existing** to launch the **Properties** options, and switch to **Layers**.
11. Set the **Color** to Moss Green, and the **Width** to **2.3 pt**, and click **Apply**. This is too heavy for this map, so we're going to modify it a little.
12. Switch to the **Structure** options and click **Add symbol layer**.
13. Switch back to **Layers**, and set the **Color** for this new layer to Apple Dust, and the **Width** to **1.8 pt** and click **Apply**. You should now have a nice line that's not too heavy, but the darker green peeking out from underneath gives it a little more weight. Save it to your styles (**Menu | Add symbol to style**). For the proposed paths, we'll reuse the symbol we just made and modify it.

14. Click the **Proposed** symbol, and from the **Gallery**, choose the symbol you just saved.
15. Switch to **Properties | Layers**.
16. Change the **Color** of the top stroke to Sahara Sand, and the bottom to cantaloupe. Click **Apply**.

By setting both categories to the same weight and style, we are telling our audience that these features are related, but the change in color will alert them that something is slightly different. Save this new symbol to your styles for quick access.

You may find that this makes your light rail harder to find. You can nudge the line weights slightly thicker, and it might also be helpful to add another layer of blue underneath, slightly wider than the rest of the line, just as we did with the bike paths in the previously mentioned steps. Remember that the goal is not to overwhelm the map with heavy lines, just to make them distinguishable from one another, as shown in the following figure:

Figure 8.7: Customizing line symbols

As with our point features, we can add in or import existing styles from the **Insert** tab on the ribbon.

Area symbols

Symbolizing area features might seem fairly basic, but there are some things we can do to customize them as well:

1. Turn on the **Historic Districts** layer, right-click it, and select **Zoom To Layer**.
2. Click the symbol in the **Contents** pane to launch the **Properties** settings in the **Symbology** pane.
3. Change the **Solid fill** layer to a **Hatched fill**, and set the **Color** to Cocoa Brown. Click **Apply**:

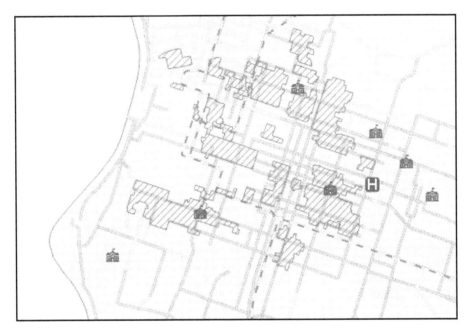

Figure 8.8: Using Hatched fill to symbolize polygons

This is one way to allow other symbol layers to show through the polygon layer, but as you can see, it's fairly noisy. Let's explore some other methods:

4. Set the layer back to **Solid fill**. Change the **Color** to Tulip Pink, and click **Apply**.

5. On the **Appearance** tab, set the **Transparency** to **75%**. This gives us a nice, subtle symbolization, so we can clearly see any features underneath, as shown in the following figure:

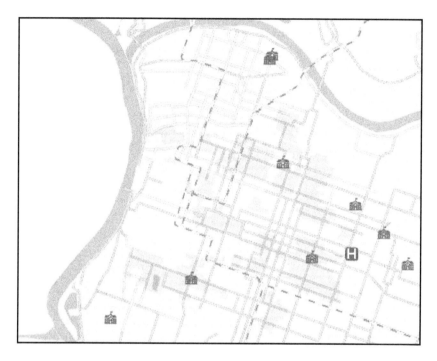

Figure 8.9: Using transparency for subtle fills

If we want to set this off a little more, we can add a more interesting border effect to focus attention.

6. Set the **Stroke fill** layer to **Gradient fill**. Leave the appearance on black to white (darker at left).
7. Change the first color to Tulip Pink, and change the second color to no color.
8. Set the interval to **25**.
9. Change the **Extent** to **Absolute**, and set the size to **4 pt**. Click **Apply**:

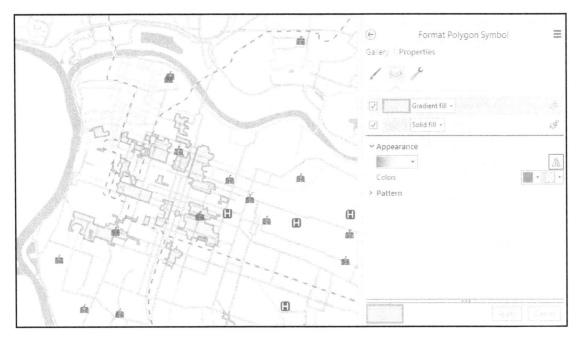

Figure 8.10: Using a Gradient fill to emphasize area features

Now we have a clear demarcation, with only minor interference with other features. For a more filled-in look, you can add a second layer to the districts and set it mostly transparent. We can also add some nice texture to areas with picture fills:

1. Turn on the **Hydro** layer.
2. Click the symbol to open the **Symbology** pane.
3. Change the **Solid fill** symbol layer to **Picture fill**.
4. Click **Picture** and browse to where you saved the files for this chapter. Select `stipple.png`.
5. Set the **Tint** to a nice dark blue, and leave the size at **8 pt**.
6. Change the **Stroke fill** layer to a light gray and click **Apply**. This probably looks a little weird where the city boundaries overlap, so we'll add a solid layer underneath.
7. Switch to **Structure**, and add a **Symbol** layer. Move it to the bottom.
8. Switch back to **Layers**, and change the fill on this layer to blue gray dust. (If this is too dark for you, remember you can change the color mode to **HSV** and lighten it.)

You should now have a nice, subtle texture in the rivers. This will give us a little visual interest without distracting from the other information. Let's do something similar for the city boundary:

1. Click the symbol for the **City Boundary** to open the **Symbology** pane.
2. Change the **Solid fill** symbol layer to **Picture fill**.
3. Click **Picture** and browse to where you saved the files for this chapter. Select `paper.jpg`, and make sure the **Quality** is set to **Picture**.
4. Add a **Tint** of light sienna, then click **Color Properties** to set the **Transparency** to **40%**.
5. Click **Reset size** to make sure the image comes in full scale, otherwise we won't see the texture. Click **Apply**:

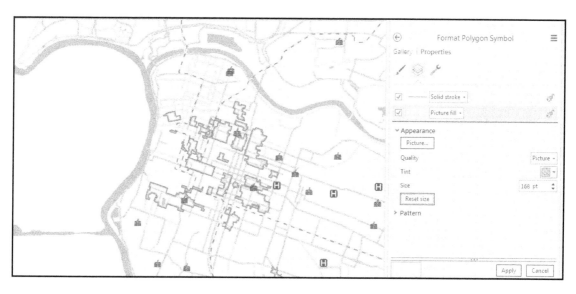

Figure 8.11: Adding Picture fills for texture

Feel free to add your own textures to area features, but don't get carried away. Too much texture, and the map is noisy. You can find textures on the internet with a quick search for tileable paper texture (be sure to check the license agreements, as with fonts), or by capturing them with a screenshot or your phone from interesting surfaces. Lighter is better, as that gives you more flexibility when adding tints. Don't forget to save your new symbols to your styles!

Classifying data

Symbolizing data isn't limited to applying graphic marks to a feature; it can refer to any method of representing the data to improve communication. Earlier, we looked at scales of measurement, which influence the type of statistical analysis techniques that can be used when analyzing data, as well as the ways in which we represent them. In general, there are more alternatives for statistical analysis when the data is quantitative, and more types of visual variables that can be applied. Remember that your map is only as good as the data that goes into it, and make sure you understand the limitations and potential error that may be already baked into it. Our job is not to magnify that error through poor representation.

Classifying the data allows us to identify patterns in the data by sorting it into buckets that will be represented in the same way. For example, equal interval divides the range between highest and lowest values into a certain number of equally-sized buckets, so if our data ranged from 0 to 100 and we wanted five classes (buckets), each class would have a span of 20, with varying numbers of observations in each (some might have none). Different situations call for different methods, and ArcGIS Pro has many options. In general, classified data is best represented with a sequential scheme, as discussed in Chapter 5, *Picking Colors with Confidence*. Darker, more intense values imply higher values of observation. The exception to this is the standard deviation method. Since the values are classified based on distance above or below the mean, it's best to use a diverging scheme, typically with a neutral color in the middle.

When classifying data, first we want to look at the extremes. What are the highest and lowest values in the dataset? A histogram will quickly reveal this, as well as other important patterns. It's also important to know whether your data has already been normalized, or if you need to normalize it yourself when setting classification parameters. Normalization can mean a number of things in the field of statistics, but in mapping it is the process of adjusting values to a baseline to make your data work across the whole map. The most common example is when working with population data; for example, if we were to make a map of people who make maps in each state, Texas and California would automatically show up as the top states, simply because there are more people there. To understand this data properly and find concentrations of cartographers, we need to normalize the data; in this case, to divide mapmakers by total population, so that we are viewing the percentage of the population who make maps, which is a much more meaningful comparison. Texas and California might still show up at or near the top, because of the high number of GIS jobs in those states, but Washington and Florida will give them a run for their money.

Let's try it out with a basic choropleth map:

1. Open the **Chapter 8** project in ArcPro.
2. Right-click on the **US States** layer and select **Symbology**.
3. In the **Symbology** pane, change the drop-down from **Single Symbol** to **Graduated Colors**.
4. Set the **Field** to **VACANT**, which is the number of vacant housing units in each state. The **Normalization** box should be automatically set to **<None>**. Leave the classification settings alone for now, and pick a sequential **Color scheme** from the drop-down:

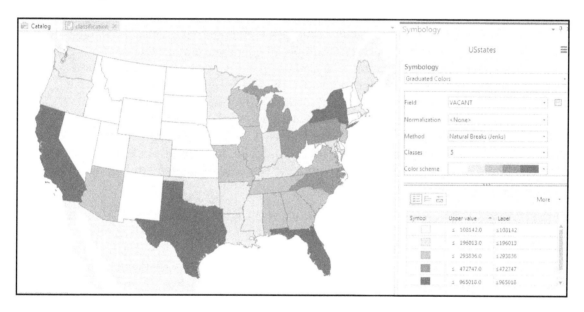

Figure 8.12: Creating a choropleth map

Notice which states stand out—California, Texas, Florida, and New York, the four most populous states. There are more homes in those states because of the higher populations, so obviously there will be more vacant ones, so this map is meaningless. To make it have value, we need to normalize the data by some attribute that will standardize how each state is represented. The population might be helpful, as more people means more houses, but there's an even better choice. There's actually a field in our table called **HSE_UNITS**, which is the total number of housing units in the state:

5. Set the **Normalization** drop-down to **HSE_UNITS**. See the difference? Now the New England states stand out, which more accurately reflects supply and demand:

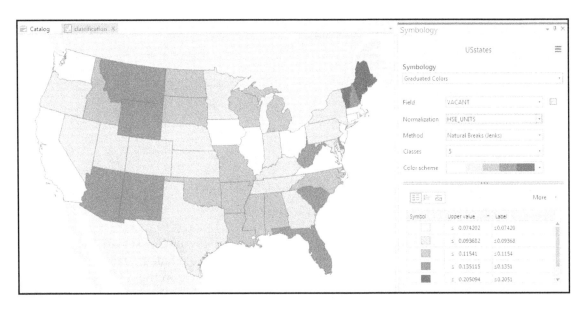

Figure 8.13: Normalizing data for proper representation

6. Click the **Menu** button at the top of the pane and select **Advanced**, then **Format Labels**.

7. Set the **Category** to **Percentage**, and select **Number represents a fraction...** to correctly format our values. You should also set the decimal places to two or fewer, so that your legend is nice and clean.

Now, let's look at how different classification methods impact the visualization. By default, ArcPro sets the classification at **Natural Breaks (Jenks)**, with **5** classes:

8. Click the back arrow at the top of the pane to return to the classification settings.

9. Click the **Histogram** button in the lower section of the pane, so we can see how the classification methods divide up the observations. With this particular dataset, **Natural Breaks (Jenks)** is fairly evenly divided in the lower values, but everything from **13.5%** up is in the final category:

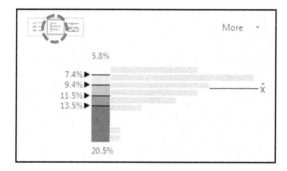

Figure 8.14: Viewing the histogram

10. Change **Method** to **Quantiles**. If we leave the number of **Classes** set on **5**, we are now looking at the values in terms of segments of the whole (recall the previous discussion). Notice how there are now more differences in the categories, and the final category now starts at 12.8% (the formatting will revert to decimal when you change classes; just reset as shown prior).

Experiment with the other classification styles, and if you're not familiar with how they work, read the descriptions in the drop-down, or check the Help files (`http://pro.arcgis.com/en/pro-app/help/mapping/layer-properties/data-classification-methods.htm`) for details. Each method has its own advantages and disadvantages, depending on both the data being displayed, and the purpose of the map you are making.

Note that if you select **Standard Deviation**, the histogram will still show the break values; but when you insert a legend, it will show the breaks in terms of standard deviations.

We can also change the number of classes, and impact the success of the map. Too few, and we oversimplify the data. Too many, and we make the distinctions between meaningless classes, and cause confusion for our readers.

Let's experiment with this setting. Watch the map and the histogram to see the changes:

11. Set the **Method** to **Equal Interval**:

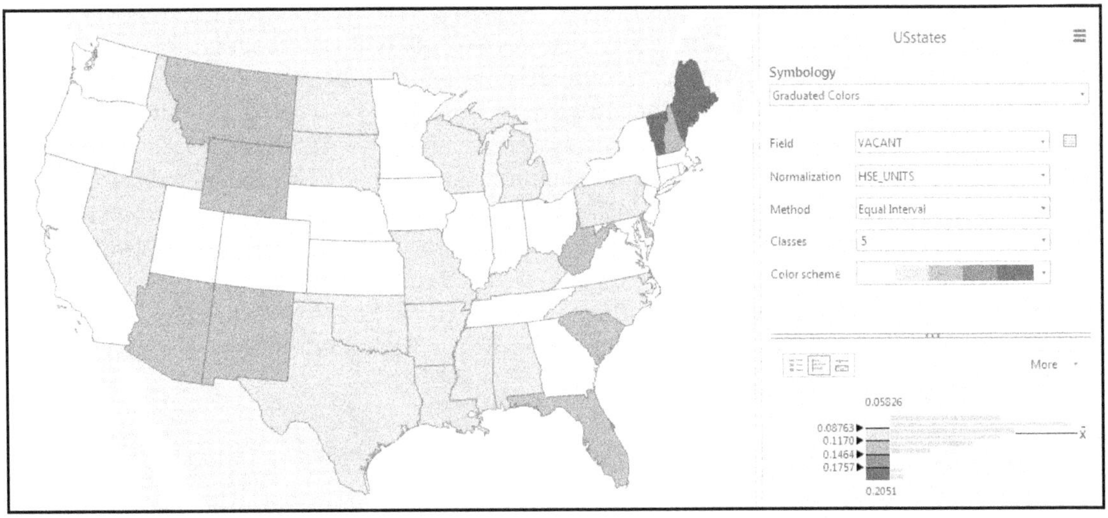

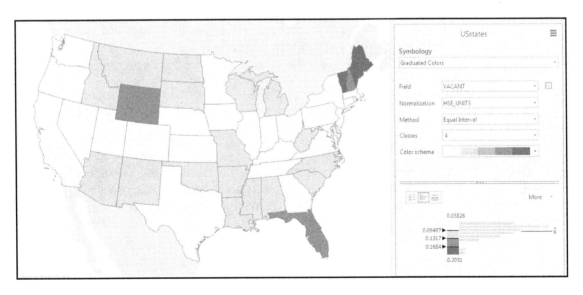

Figure 8.15: Equal interval with five classes

12. Change **Classes** from **5** to **4**. Notice how that flattens out the variation in most of the country:

Figure 8.16: Equal interval with four classes

4 classes brings out a couple of states changing it to **7** gives us a little more detail on what's happening in New England, but we need to decide if that's really useful.

It's important not to select more than seven classes, especially if your sequential color ramp is a single color, as the human eye has trouble distinguishing more shades than that. Sure, we can see them in the legend when they are neatly arranged, but trying to match the shades from the map to the legend becomes more challenging with more classes, especially in ranges of common color acuity issues (as seen in `Chapter 5`, *Picking Colors with Confidence*), such as reds and greens. This is why five classes is the default, and you should use caution when selecting more than that, if your audience actually needs to distinguish values. But what about when we are setting classes on a continuous dataset like temperature, where only approximate values are important? Feel free to turn it all the way to 11 (or 32, which is the maximum), and get a beautiful, graduated pattern.

Proportional and graduated symbols

Symbols are sized based on data values, rather than arbitrary assignment. In Arc's terminology, graduated is equivalent to range grading (classifying), and proportional is equivalent to absolute scaling (individual representation). Graduated symbols can be classified using any of the methods discussed earlier, and the size of the symbol is set by specifying a top and bottom size.

This type of symbology can be used to represent point features, placed at the location of the feature; however, by creating feature centroids, we can also use it to represent areas as points. In this case, it's best if there is a significant variation in the data, as homogenous data yields too many similar-sized symbols, and therefore leaves us with a very boring map.

Much like the interaction of color, neighboring symbols can have an impact on our perception of size, so this needs to be considered carefully as well. The addition of subtle lines in the background can often help control this effect.

We are also notoriously bad at estimating relative circle sizes. If we compare two circles side by side, rather than accurately estimate that one is five times larger, we mentally try to fit five of the smaller circles into the larger one, which doesn't work. To correct this, we can use Flannery's Compensation, a calculation that draws symbols by apparent scaling, rather than absolute scaling, and makes the circles look right.

Be careful not to get too creative with proportional symbols. Simple shapes, such as basic geometric forms, are the easiest for us to interpret, while more complex symbols make it more difficult for us to perceive differences in size. Let's practice with some sample data:

1. Open the **European Wine** Map in the **Chapter 8** project.
2. In the **Contents** pane, click the symbol for the **EuroMedWine** layer to open the **Symbology** pane.
3. Change the **Symbology** to **Proportional Symbols**, and set the field to **AvgGal**. France, Italy, and Spain stand out, as we might expect.
4. To exclude countries that don't produce any wine, click the **Menu** button in the upper-right of the pane and select **Advanced**. Under **Data exclusion**, add the clause **AvgGal is Equal to 0** and click **Apply**:
    - This will automatically add an excluded values color to your map, so if you don't want this, on the main **Symbology** pane, click **More**, and uncheck **Show excluded values**.
5. Just as with our choropleth, we want to consider normalizing the data; in this case, we'll look at production per hectare. Set **Normalization** to **Viny1000Ha**, which represents the number of vineyards in thousands of hectares.
6. Set the color and size using the **Template**, and **Minimum** and **Maximum** size settings. If you want to use Flannery's Compensation, set the **Maximum** size to **None**, and then check the box.

Proportional symbol mapping will place the symbol, whatever it is, at the center of a particular country. When you set up your map, Europe should (obviously) be at the center, but this leaves us with a problem. Some countries, like Russia and the countries on the North Coast of Africa, may have their symbols placed out of view. Instead of expanding your view extent, you can move these points by using the following Arc functions (first, make sure to create a bookmark so you can quickly return to your current view extent):

- **Feature to Point** tool: Use your countries layer as the input feature and leave all other options as the defaults. This will produce a point feature with the same attribute information, as the polygons; symbolize it as described previously instead of the original polygon layer.
- **Edit point locations:** Switch to **List by Selection** in the **Contents** pane. Turn off everything except your points layer. On the **Edit** ribbon, click **Modify** in the **Features** section. Choose the **Move** tool and select a point you want to move, and move them to where you will be able to see them at your bookmarked view extent. On the **Edit** ribbon, click **Save**. You can do as many iterations of this process as you need to get the points in the correct locations. It may also be easier to do this before setting the points to proportional symbols.

To use graduated symbols instead, change the **Symbology** to **Graduated Symbols**, and then use the techniques discussed earlier with our choropleth map for setting classification methods and the number of classes. One sample result is shown in *Figure 8.18*.

Making symbols dynamic

Map readers interact with maps in more ways than we ever imagined just a few years ago. As they zoom, pan, shrink, or enlarge to plan routes, create reports, or display them on large screens, it's important for the design elements we have selected to be responsive to those changes. ArcGIS Pro has the ability to respond to changes in size or underlying data with ease.

Controlling visibility at scale

As the scale of our map changes, the level of generalization or abstraction must also change. For small-scale maps, we might represent a city with a circle; but at a large scale, it may be more appropriate to show the city boundaries. Rather than make several different maps, we can take advantage of ArcGIS Pro's ability to control visibility based on the scale at which the map is being viewed.

In our map of Sacramento, our symbol choices look pretty good up-close, but if we zoom out to the whole city, the school and hospital symbols are overwhelming, and we can barely see the historic districts. With ArcGIS Pro, we can modify the symbols based on the current scale of the map, similar to the zoom level controls you'll work with in Chapter 9, *Getting Started with ArcGIS Online*:

1. Open the **Chapter 8** project and select the **Sacramento** map.
2. Select the **Sacramento bookmark** to zoom to that scale, and notice how overwhelming our point symbols are.
3. Click the **public schools** symbol to open the **Symbology** pane, and switch to **Properties | Symbol**.
4. Above the **Appearance** option, check the box next to **Enable scale-based sizing**. Click **Apply**.
5. The **Sacramento bookmark** is approximately 1:200,000, so we'll set a size stop just beyond that to control the size. Drag the left-hand size stop to 1:500,000. With it still selected (dark), set the size to **11 pt**.
6. Click **Apply**, and the symbols should shrink to a manageable size.
7. Repeat for the **hospitals** layer, setting the size to **7 pt**.

If we are making a print map, we'll need to make sure our legend symbols are created at the correct bookmark level, so they are the same size. We can also choose to make a layer visible or not visible at certain scales, using the settings under **Properties**, as shown in the following screenshot:

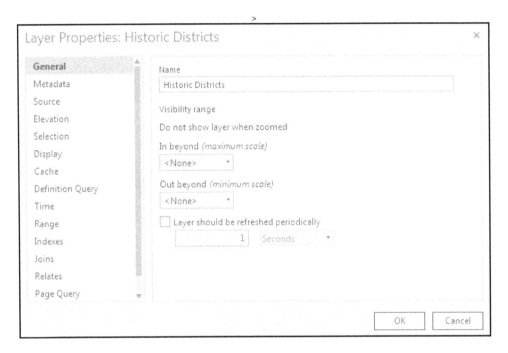

Figure 8.17: Setting layer visibility

Attribute-driven symbology

ArcPro also gives us the ability to control symbols by attribute even more dynamically. In addition to setting the symbol based on some attribute in the table (for example, size, or type), we can also vary size (if appropriate) and **Transparency** by any numeric attribute. These options can be found under the **Menu button | Vary symbology by attribute**. Options will vary based on feature type and data values. For example, we could return to our **European Wine** Map and alter the way we show production by hectare. In the example shown in the following figure, symbol transparency is set to **Vary** by **AvgGal**, so that countries with more total production will have less transparent symbols.

This minimizes the visual impact of those large circles in Central Europe, yet leaves them legible so the data is still being communicated:

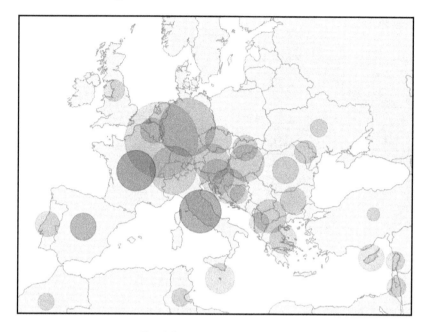

Figure 8.18: Varying transparency by attribute

Attribute-driven symbology gives you more flexibility when symbolizing complex data, either to reinforce information with redundant coding, add in additional variables as above, or blend datasets, such as in our election map in Chapter 5, *Picking Colors with Confidence.*

Practicing on your own

Return to the election map data from Chapter 5, *Picking Colors with Confidence.* Use **Vary symbology by attribute** to set each layer to increase **Transparency** based on population or total votes, and see what happens. Or, use your own data, and experiment.

Summary

Symbolization is a critical part of map communication, and effective use of symbols can make or break your map. In this chapter, we learned about the scales at which data is measured, and how that impacts the visual variables we can use to display it. We also learned how to work with classification methods, and how to use attribute-driven symbology to include additional attributes.

In the next chapter, we'll use these tools and our saved styles, as we move into ArcGIS Online. We'll also collaborate, share, and distribute maps and data within our organization, or with the world. For further information, you may refer to Jacques Bertin (1967), *Semiologie Graphique, Esri Press* (2010).

9
Getting Started with ArcGIS Online

So far in this book, you have been doing GIS with ArcGIS Pro, which is a desktop software package. GIS has quickly expanded into the web, as it allows the sharing of GIS data without the need for complex desktop software. The web is the future of GIS and it is necessary to understand web GIS to keep yourself up to date. Esri, the maker of ArcGIS Pro, also has a powerful web GIS platform that ties into ArcGIS Pro. In this chapter, you will learn the basics of ArcGIS Online and how you can share your data and create great cartographic products that live online, accessible to the world. This chapter will be a high-level overview of ArcGIS Online, as a whole book could be written about it. You will learn important concepts about ArcGIS Online and how to perform simple tasks, but it is recommended to do more in-depth training in ArcGIS Online. Esri has provided a great set of step-by-step tutorials on how to perform tasks in ArcGIS Online, available at `https://doc.arcgis.com/en/arcgis-online/`.

Since you are using ArcGIS Pro, it is assumed that you have an account with ArcGIS Online already. If you don't have access to an ArcGIS Online account, you can start a free 21 day trial that gives you access and the ability to publish to ArcGIS Online at `https://www.esri.com/arcgis/trial`; or, if you want to use ArcGIS Online for more than 21 days, you can sign up for a free developer account at `https://developers.arcgis.com/sign-up`. However, there are rules you have to follow in using these free accounts. You cannot use them for production/paid work, as they are simply for testing ArcGIS Online.

In this chapter, we will cover the following topics:

- How to navigate ArcGIS Online
- How to add layers into your web map and change its symbolization
- How to upload data from ArcGIS Pro to ArcGIS Online

ArcGIS Online

Web GIS is an implementation of modern GIS and has been around for many years, but has had exponential growth recently. It was once only found within large organizations and governments, because web GIS required complex **relational database management systems** (**RDBMS**), GIS, **Hypertext Transfer Protocol** (**HTTP**) server software, the hardware to run them, and the people to maintain these systems. With the emergence of cloud architecture, individuals and organizations can now deploy a web GIS without having to manage all the overhead. Esri created a web GIS platform called ArcGIS Online that is hosted in the cloud and is fully integrated into ArcGIS Pro. ArcGIS Online also provides preconfigured web apps that tie into your data or other data found in ArcGIS Online. It also provides what's called the **Web App Builder**, which allows you to customize your own web mapping application and deploy it through ArcGIS Online or your own website.

The components of ArcGIS Online

Before you dive into ArcGIS Online, it is important to understand the infrastructure that makes up ArcGIS Online. ArcGIS Online is currently hosted in the **Amazon Web Services** (**AWS**) platform. This allows ArcGIS Online to be easily accessible, fast, and scalable. While you don't need to know how exactly ArcGIS Online is technically structured in AWS, it is important to understand that there are three tiers that make up ArcGIS Online—the data tier, the GIS tier, and the web tier. Each of these tiers plays an important role in how data is shown in ArcGIS Online and each will now be explained.

Data tier

The **data tier** is where your GIS and non-GIS data is stored and maintained. The data tier is essentially an RDMS, like Oracle, Microsoft SQL, or PostgreSQL, and is stored as tables or blobs. This tier allows you to store and query the data in a multitude of ways. However, you don't have any control in this tier, as it is completely managed by Esri.

GIS tier

The **GIS tier** is how you expose the GIS data you have stored in the data tier. Typically, within an organization or government, this was handled by what is called ArcGIS Server. The GIS tier exposes **Representational State Transfer** (**REST**) services to be consumed by a web application such as ArcGIS Online.

Web tier

The **web tier** is the frontend of ArcGIS Online. It is the web application that consumes the REST services from the GIS tier. In ArcGIS Online, the web tier has three parts—data management, data visualization, and apps. You will get a more in-depth explanation about these three parts as we proceed further.

Web GIS services

The **web GIS services** are served out of the GIS tier of ArcGIS Online, which you learned about in the previous section. These services come in four types of layers—feature layer, tile layer, scene layer, and elevation layer. Each one of these layer types exposes different functionality to interact with the data. We will look at each layer type in depth as follows:

- Feature layer
- Tile layer
- Scene layer
- Elevation layer

Feature layer

The **feature layer** is the most common type of layer in ArcGIS Online. It is a service that allows the querying, visualization, and editing of your vector GIS data. Compared to the desktop environment of ArcGIS Pro, this would be your point, line, or polygon feature class layer from a geodatabase in your map. With the feature layer, you can select features, apply queries, configure pop-ups, and even create views based on the feature layer.

Tile layer

The **tile layer** is a fast-loading layer that is made up of pre-made tiles of your data. Tile layers break up your GIS data into small chunks so it has faster display speed. The practice of creating and serving out tiles rather than a layer's geometry has been standard in the major online mapping companies. A normal tile layer is a raster end product, meaning vector GIS data is converted into images. While this increases the speed of drawing a map, it does make symbology choices somewhat permanent. If you wanted to change the symbology of the tile layer, you have to regenerate all the tiles again.

Luckily, in the past couple of years, a new type of tile has been developed that can help solve this problem—a vector tile layer. A vector tile layer is much like a standard raster tile layer, but instead of the end product being a raster, the tile is made up of the vector GIS data you published. Because the end product is vector, you can change the symbology on the fly to suit your needs.

Scene layer

For years, 3D has been slowly creeping into the GIS industry, and with ArcGIS Pro and ArcGIS Online there is an easy way of creating and sharing 3D data. The **scene layer** is a 3D GIS data layer that is rendered as vector tiles and can be viewed in 3D in ArcGIS Online.

Elevation layer

The **elevation layer** is a raster layer that is served as raster tiles, but instead of showing layers of vector based GIS data, the elevation layer shows a continuous surface representing elevation. The elevation layer is used in 3D scenes on ArcGIS Online, so you can bring in your own ground model if the one provided by Esri is not sufficient.

ArcGIS Online overview

As mentioned at the beginning of this chapter, ArcGIS Online is a web GIS that is housed in the cloud. ArcGIS Online is a GIS ecosystem that houses many organizations. In the context of ArcGIS Online, an organization is a paid membership group. While a lot of ArcGIS Online is free and open to anyone, you will need an account that is a member of an organization with the right level, role, and privilege to create and edit GIS data and apps. Accounts, organizations, levels, roles, and privileges can be a bit confusing to someone who hasn't used ArcGIS Online before; you will find quick summaries of each as follows.

Accounts

Everything you do in ArcGIS Online is tied to your account. Your account carries around your identity in the ArcGIS Online ecosystem, and depending on the account type and privileges given to your account, your experience will be different.

Public account

If you don't have a paid organizational account, you can still create a free account with ArcGIS Online, called a **public account**. The public account gives you the ability to carry your identity with you within the ArcGIS Online ecosystem and allows you to create, save, and share web maps, as well as upload limited types of files to store and share. You can create a public account by signing up with an email address or by signing up via social media like Google or Facebook at `https://www.arcgis.com/home/createaccount.html`.

Organizational account

The **organizational account** type is one that is a member of a paid organization. An organizational account can be created for you, or you can convert your public account into an organizational account if approved by the organization's administrator. With the organizational account, you will have the ability to create, edit, and share GIS data, web maps, and apps. However, what your organizational account has privileges to do is defined in your role.

Levels, roles, and privileges

An ArcGIS Online organization can create and share GIS data, web maps, apps, and other items, and the organization has the ability to control the access of these things through levels, roles, and privileges. Each one of these settings has increasing customization, which is explained as follows.

Levels

The **level** of your account is what distinguishes it as a viewer or something more complex. There are currently two levels in ArcGIS Online—Level 1 and Level 2. Level 1 is a viewer type role that only has privileges to view content shared only to the organization, as well as groups they are a member of. This means they cannot save anything or create data. Level 2 is for accounts that need to be able to view, create, and edit GIS data, as well as create and own groups within the organization.

Roles

Roles are set lists of privileges given to an account and can only be applied to Level 2 accounts. There are four default roles that come built in to ArcGIS Online—viewer, user, publisher, and administrator. A viewer is much like a Level 1 account in that they cannot create anything, but can have access to geoprocessing tools like geocoding and routing. A user is a role that allows the account to add items, edit GIS data, and create and share web maps and apps within the organization, as well as create groups. The publisher role gives all the privileges that are granted to the viewer and user roles, in addition to the ability to publish GIS data as services and perform spatial analysis. The administrator role has all the privileges found in ArcGIS Online and can administer the organization as they see fit. In addition to these four roles, the organization administrator can create custom roles if there is a need to specifically limit or grant certain functionality to accounts.

Privileges

Privileges are the finest control an ArcGIS Online administrator has in restricting accounts in their organization. There are many privileges within ArcGIS Online; here are a few, so that you can have a high-level understanding of privileges: the ability to join a group, edit features, perform analysis, create content, and use demographic data. There are quite a few privileges; too many to list out here—so if you would like to learn more about privileges, as well as the roles and levels, visit `https://doc.arcgis.com/en/arcgis-online/reference/roles.htm`.

The organization

Now that you have had a quick overview of the GIS data that can be served out of ArcGIS Online and what specific types of accounts can or cannot do in ArcGIS Online, it's time to go over what ArcGIS Online looks like within your organization.

In the following figure, you can see a typical organization account home page:

Figure 9.1: Default ArcGIS organization landing page

An organization has seven areas within it: Home, Gallery, Map, Scene, Groups, Content, and Organization. Here's a quick overview of each area:

- **Home**: This is the home page for the organization. It can be customized to give a specific look and feel to match the owning organization.
- **Gallery**: This area is where you can search for and discover content in your organization or throughout all of ArcGIS Online.
- **Map**: The web map within ArcGIS Online to view GIS data.
- **Scene**: The 3D scene viewer to view 2D and 3D content in a 3D environment.
- **Groups**: This area contains the groups you own or are a member of.
- **Content**: This area shows all of your own content in ArcGIS Online.
- **Organization**: This area is the administration area of the organization, where accounts can be added and removed; levels, roles, and privileges can be managed; many other administration tools exist.

These seven areas can be found along the top of ArcGIS Online when you are logged into an organization, except when in the web map or scene viewer, where they will be in a collapsed menu on the top-left corner. An in-depth review of each area is detailed as follows.

Gallery

When you access the gallery area of ArcGIS Online, you get two tabs—your organization's featured content and Esri's featured content. The content that is shown in your organization's featured content is content that your organization administrator has chosen to be featured to everyone that is a part of the organization, or to the public, if your organization is shared publicly. The Esri featured content is the Living Atlas content that Esri wants to promote:

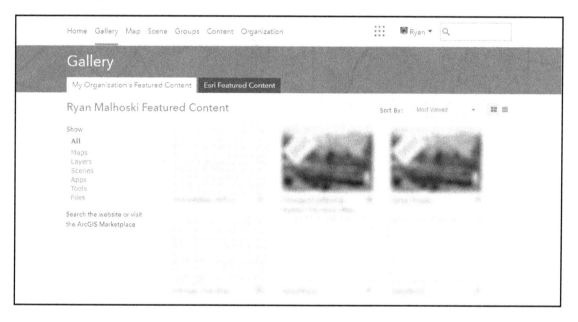

Figure 9.2: Gallery view of an ArcGIS Online organization

Map

When you view the web map area of your organization, you are presented with the web map showing the default world topographic base map, shown as follows:

Figure 9.3: ArcGIS Online web map

To the left of the map is the **Details** pane, showing information about the web map, the layer controls of the web map, and the legend of the web map. Just above the map and the **Details** pane is a grey bar with icons and a **Search** bar. These icons allow you to do a multitude of things to your web map and each is described as follows:

- **Add**: Allows you to add data to your map. The following are the different ways you can add data to your map:
    - **Search for layers**: When you click this option, the pane to the left of the map will change and show a **Search** dialog. From here you can choose to search just your organization's data, search through an ArcGIS server somewhere else, search all of ArcGIS Online, search Esri's Living Atlas layers, search your favorites, or search your own content, through the drop-down menu. You'll notice there are two checkboxes below the drop-down menu. The first allows you to only search for data that is within your current map extent. The second allows you to search only **authoritative data,** which is a new feature Esri just added. When you have found a layer you would like to add to your web map, just click **Add text** to the right of the item.
    - **Browse Living Atlas layers**: When you click this option, a window will appear where you can search through Esri's curated **Living Atlas** data. In previous exercises in this book, you have utilized data from **Living Atlas**. To add this data, click **Add to map** below the thumbnail.

- **Add layer from web**: This option is for when you want to add data from another GIS server hosted somewhere on the web. When you click this option, a window will appear asking what type of data you are referencing—an ArcGIS server, **Open Geospatial Consortium** (**OGC**) web services, a KML file, a geoRSS file, or a CSV file hosted on a web server. Underneath the URL box there is a check back to determine whether you would like the layer you are adding to be a basemap.
    - **Add layer from file**: This option is what you would use if you wanted to upload data from your computer and add it to your map. Examples of this are a zipped shapefile, CSV or TXT with locations in commas, semi-colons, or a tab delimited format, GPX files from a GPS unit, and GeoJSON.
    - **Add map notes**: This option creates a new layer where you can create a layer specifically for notes and drawings on the map. There are a few templates for symbology for notes for specific purposes.
- **Basemap**: Allows you to change the basemap in your web map. By default, these are limited to the Esri raster basemaps, but your administrator can add more if needed.
- **Analysis**: Allows you to perform specific geoprocessing tasks using data in your web map, like summarizing data, calculating density, or creating drive time areas.
- **Save**: Save your web map, or save as, creating a copy of your web map.
- **Share**: Using this tool, you can set the sharing properties for your web map, get a shortened URL to send to others, get the ability to share to social media, generate the HTML of your web map to embed in another website or blog, or create a web app from the map.
- **Print**: Using this tool, you can generate a map suitable for printing or conversion to another document type, such as a PDF. You have two options—with or without legend.
- **Directions**: This tool will generate directions from one location to one or multiple stops, including turn-by-turn directions and travel time and add the route to the web map. You can also change the transportation type for your directions.
- **Measure**: This tool allows you to measure the area or the line you draw on the map, with the ability to convert to different units on the fly. You can also generate a latitude/longitude or **degrees**, **minutes**, **seconds** (**DMS**) coordinate with a click on the map.

- **Bookmarks**: This tool stores bookmarks you create in the web map. In a bookmark, you can store the zoom and extent of your web map so that you can easily jump between extents.
- **Search** bar: This search bar utilizes Esri's world geocoder service, which can search addresses, cities, landmarks, business names, and postal codes in more than 100 countries around the world. You can also input lat/long and DMS coordinates into this.

Scene

The **scene viewer** is a 3D environment for your GIS data. When you first visit the scene viewer, you are given a choice of creating a new scene or loading some Esri curated example scenes. The navigational controls for a scene can be confusing at first, but the left mouse button handles panning, while the right mouse button handles tilting the scene:

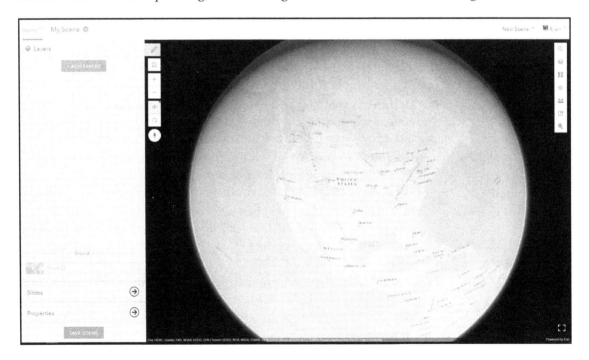

Figure 9.4: ArcGIS Online scene viewer

The scene controls on the scene viewer are very similar to the web map viewer, but instead of being across the top, they are split between the left pane and the top-right corner of the scene viewer:

- Left pane:
    - **Add Layers**: You can search for content or enter a layer URL at the bottom
    - **Slides**: They are bookmarks in the scene viewer and have the same capabilities as bookmarks in a web map
    - **Properties**: Where you can change the thumbnail, title, summary, and tags of your scene
- Top-right toolbar (top to bottom):
    - **Search**: It functions similar to the **Search** option in the preceding *Map* section. You can also input lat/long and DMS coordinates into this.
    - **Layers/Legend**: The layer control for your scene, as well as the legend.
    - **Basemap**: Allows you to change the basemap in your web map. By default, these are limited to the Esri raster basemaps, but your administrator can add more if needed.
    - **Daylight**: A tool that will show the lighting conditions, given no clouds, for any time, in any day. This can be set to **Play** so you can see shadows cast by 3D features move quickly through the day.
    - **Measure**: This tool allows you to measure a line across the scene, showing the distance in direct or horizontal and the change in vertical. You can change the units on the fly in this tool, as well.
    - **Share**: Using this tool, you can set the sharing properties for your scene, get a shortened URL to send to others, get the ability to share to social media, generate the HTML of your scene to embed in another website or blog, or create a web app from the scene.
    - **Settings**: With this tool, you can set the rendering performance to run for higher quality or quicker performance. You can also see and set the mouse navigation to two settings—default and ArcGIS Pro.

Groups

This is where you can find the groups that you are a member of and groups that you own. You can see featured groups, which is a list of groups curated by your organization administrator. You can also see all of the groups within your organization. A **group** is a collection of items that share a common theme or specific area of interest. These groups can be used to restrict access to certain members or allow items shared to that group to be edited by members of the group:

Figure 9.5: ArcGIS Online groups

Content

The **content** area is where you do your data management. As mentioned in the `Chapter 1`, *How Maps Get Made*, data management is very important to a well-functioning GIS. ArcGIS Online visually organizes your data in a folder system in the content area. Everything you create or upload in ArcGIS Online is stored in your content area.

On the left side of the content area, you will see the list of your folders, including the root, which is signified by a small blue house next to your username:

Figure 9.6: ArcGIS Online content tab

In ArcGIS online, you cannot create sub-folders, meaning you can only go one level deep. The term item refers to any piece of information, no matter the type. For example: a layer, a web map, and a web app are three items. When creating or adding an item, it is required to put in at least one tag. But it is best practice to add as many descriptive tags as possible, to make it easier to discover.

The following are the four tabs found in the content area:

- **My Content**: A list of all the items you own in ArcGIS Online
- **My Favorites**: A list of all the items in ArcGIS Online that you have favorited
- **My Groups**: A list of all the items from the groups that you own or are a member of
- **My Organization**: A list of all the items from your organization

The following are the items in the left pane area of **My Content**:

- **Add Item**: From here, you have four options for adding an item into your ArcGIS Online account:
    - **From my computer**: Choose a file from your computer to add to ArcGIS Online. The data does not have to be GIS in nature; for example, you can add images, PDFs, a PowerPoint project, and many more. For a full list of items you can add, click the small blue circle with the question mark in it, near the top middle of the window.
    - **From the web**: From this window, you can add an ArcGIS server or other OGC GIS service like you can in a web map, but this allows you to save the item for use across all your web maps or web apps in ArcGIS Online.

This will not copy any data over, as it is only a reference to the original data source.

    - **From cloud drive**: From this window, you can add data from a cloud based file drive such as Google Drive, Dropbox, or OneDrive.
    - **An application**: You can add an already existing app to your content using this option. You may need to fill out some information about the application, such as its purpose and the API type it's using. Again, this won't copy any data, as it is only a reference.
- **Create**: From this, you can create new items that you host locally and control:
    - **Feature Layer**: Create a new feature layer, where you can choose from a set of templates Esri has provided, copy the schema from an existing layer in your organization, or copy from a URL to a feature service.
    - **Tile Layer**: You can create a tile layer from an existing feature layer that you already have in ArcGIS Online.

Warning: Creating a tile layer is not free!

- **Map**: Create a new web map.
- **Scene**: Create a new scene.
- **Locator** (**view**): Create a view of the Esri world geocoder set to a custom extent or to remove landmarks or other items so they will not show in searches.
- **App using a template**: Create an app using a list of Esri provided templates.
- **App using Web AppBuilder**: Create an app using a Bare Bones app, where you can configure it as you wish.
- **App using Operations Dashboard**: Create a new operations dashboard for use in real-time operations.

- **Folders**: You can create a new folder by clicking **New**, next to folders, then naming your new folder. You can also filter the list in the left pane by performing a search in your list and only displaying results.
- Below **Folders** are five accordion menus that allow you to filter your data in the main central pane, based on the criteria found in each accordion menu. For example, you can filter out just layers modified in the last 30 days, shared with your organization, that are authoritative. To activate a filter, click it, and to deactivate it, click it again.

The central pane is where your items are displayed. It shows you the title of the item, the type of item, a symbol showing its shared status, a star to indicate if it's a favorite, the last modified date, and three dots (ellipses) to open a menu of more options that are dependent on the type of item. At the top of the central pane there is a **Search** bar where you can search for items and display only the results.

Organization

The **organization** area is where administrators can manage the organization. Here, they can change the settings to fit the organization's needs, as well as manage accounts within the organization. In this area, you can also see the organization's subscription status:

Figure 9.7: ArcGIS Online organization tab.

 Not every user can see the organization area. It is dependent on how the organization administrator has set up the organization.

The item description page

Each item within ArcGIS Online has a standardized description page called the **Item Description** page. This page can be slightly different, based on the type of item you are looking at. The following is an example of a feature layer I created, which you will create in a later exercise:

Figure 9.8: ArcGIS Online item description page

What this page shows you is a thumbnail, summary, description, and other details about the item. The long rectangular boxes near the top-right corner of the page give you options to interact with the item. These options are pretty descriptive, so we won't go into detail about each one. What was not captured in the preceding figure were a few more pieces of information about the item, which can be seen underneath. The most important piece of information are the tags associated with the item. Tags are descriptive words about the item that are searchable. This makes it easier for others to discover data within ArcGIS Online. It is recommended to have at least three tags for an item, but more is always better:

Figure 9.9: ArcGIS Online item metadata area

Web maps

The main purpose of ArcGIS Online is to display your GIS data within the web browser. You display your GIS data through the web map viewer in ArcGIS Online, found in the map area. The **web map** is a JavaScript based web map that utilizes Esri's JavaScript API, so it can be viewed on not just computers, but mobile devices, as well. The web map can show lots of different kinds of GIS data and has the ability to control different settings for layers, like transparency, symbology, pop-ups, or even filtering data based off queries. What you can or cannot do to a layer is based on what type of layer it is. In the *Web GIS services* section, you learned about the different kinds of GIS services, that can be layers in your web map. The following are the typical controls for a feature layer in a web map:

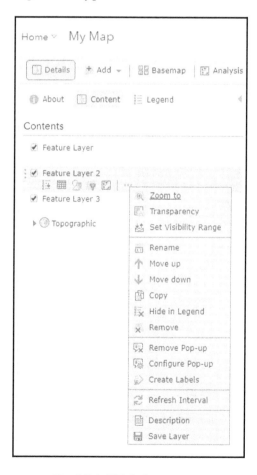

Figure 9.10: ArcGIS Online feature layer menu

Here is a quick run through of each tool in the layer management tool set, starting from the left and moving right, then down the drop-down menu:

- **Legend**: Create a legend of the layer
- **Attribute Table**: Open the attribute table of the layer, which will appear from the bottom
- **Symbology**: Change the symbology of the layer
- **Filter**: Using standardized queries, filter the layer to show a selection of the layer
- **Perform Analysis**: Perform spatial analysis on the layer
- **Zoom to**: Zoom to the full extent of the layer
- **Transparency**: Modify the transparency of the layer
- **Set Visibility Range**: Set the visible extent of the layer
- **Rename**: Rename the layer.

This only changes the name of the layer inside the web map; it will not change the name of the layer as it is stored.

- **Move up/Move down**: Change the order of the layer so it will draw above or below other layers.

You can also click, hold, and drag layers to reorder them.

- **Copy**: Create a copy of the layer within the web map
- **Hide in Legend**: Hide this layer from the web map legend
- **Remove**: Remove the layer from the web map
- **Remove Pop-up**: Enable/Remove Pop-up, turns pop-ups for the layer on or off
- **Configure Pop-up**: Bring up a window so you can configure the pop-ups for the layer
- **Create Labels**: Create labels for your layer
- **Refresh Interval**: Used for live datasets, to set an interval when new data will be pulled in
- **Description**: Open a new window to show the item description page for the layer
- **Save Layer**: Save any changes you have made to the layer to the item, or, if it's not your item, it will create a new item in your content

Not all of these options are available for each type of layer, so don't be surprised if you don't see all these tools available in your web map.

Publishing a GIS service and creating a web map

Now that you have had a thorough review of the ArcGIS Online ecosystem, it's time to get hands-on by publishing a feature layer and creating a web map using it. You will upload a feature class of the census tracts in Sacramento County, California, showing the percent of income paid for rent and symbolize it in ArcGIS Online with a diverging color ramp, using the skills you learned in Chapter 5, *Picking Colors with Confidence*. The goal is to show where rent as a percentage of income is above the standard 33%:

1. Open ArcGIS Pro and open the Chapter9.aprx project, and you will see one polygon feature called **RentPercentOfIncomeSacramentoACS2016**. This polygon layer shows the census tracts for California, and, in the data table, shows two fields: **RentPercentage** and **Error**.

2. Make sure your active portal is set to ArcGIS Online. To do this, click your name in the top-right corner of ArcGIS Pro and make sure that under your name, you see https://www.arcgis.com; if it says something else, click **Manage Portals** and select or add https://www.arcgis.com, and log in with your organizational account.

3. Since we can handle the symbolization and other finishing touches in ArcGIS Online, you don't need to do anything to the layer. Right-click **RentPercentOfIncomeSacramentoACS2016** in the **Contents** pane and click **Share As Web Layer**.

4. The **Share As Web Layer** pane should appear on the right. Leave the name as **RentPercentOfIncomeSacramentoACS2016** and set the **Layer Type** to **Feature**. You'll notice that the **Summary** and **Tags** have already been filled in. This is because ArcGIS Pro is reading the metadata of the feature class and populating the fields with the metadata. Under **Sharing Options,** leave it so **My Content** is the only checkbox selected.

5. Near the top of the **Share As Web Layer** pane, you can see three words separated by bars—**General, Configuration,** and **Content. General** is the current active menu you are in; click on **Configuration** and look through the settings. Since we do not need to edit this data currently, we don't need to enable editing. **Enable Sync** allows someone to download a version of your data to use offline and can upload changes to the master dataset. We don't need this, so leave it unchecked.

Export Data allows someone to export your data if they want. Leave this unchecked right now, as we can change this once it's on ArcGIS Online. Leave the other properties as they are. The **Content** menu shows you what content will be uploaded to ArcGIS Online.

6. Now that we have configured the settings for the web layer, click **Publish**. You will see a blue bar scroll by at the bottom of the **Share As Web Layer** pane, and it will tell you what it is currently doing. This upload should not take more than a couple of minutes, depending on your internet speed.

7. When the layer has successfully been published, you'll see green text at the bottom of the **Share As Web Layer** pane saying **Manage Web Layer**. This is a hyperlink to your new item in ArcGIS Online; click it, and it should open your web browser and take you to the item description page. You may need to log in.

8. Your web browser should be showing the item description page for the web layer you just created. Take a moment to look at all the options on this page. You can see the text that we saw in ArcGIS Pro show up in the **Summary** area; it shows the type of item below the **Summary**, it shows us the layer below the description, and the tags can be found in the bottom-right of the page. For this exercise, we won't go through all the options and menus, but after the exercise, it is recommended to do some exploring.

9. From the item description page, click the blue bar that says **Open in Map Viewer**. This will open a new web map with your layer placed inside of it. You can see that the data is symbolized with just a black outline. We want to change this to show a diverging color ramp based off an attribute value.

10. For this exercise, you want to symbolize the **RentPercentage** field. To do this, hover your mouse over the **RentPercentOfIncomeACS2016** and click the **Change Style tool,** which is symbolized with a circle, square, and triangle. The left pane will change, and in the drop-down menu under **Choose an Attribute to Show,** select **RentPercentage**. You'll notice that the layer in the map has changed to show a color ramp. Under **Select a drawing style**, click **Options** under **Counts and Amounts (Color)**.

11. The pane should have changed again, and you should see a histogram with sliders and your default color ramp. Since you are showing a divergent dataset, you want to change the **Theme** to **Above and Below**. To change the color of the ramp, click **Symbols** on the right. This should open a new window showing pre-built color ramps. Look through them and choose one that you like. To invert the color ramp, click the two arrows in a circle below your ramp. You can also change the outline by selecting **outline** and choosing your preferred settings. Once you have the ramp you like, click **OK**.

12. You'll notice the color of your ramp has change to the one you chose and there are three sliders. Move the middle slider so it shows **33**. You'll notice the other two sliders move with it. Leave the other sliders alone and click **OK,** then click **Done**.

13. Now, to make it easier for someone to interact with your map, you'll want to configure the pop-ups for your layer. Click anywhere within your data, and you'll notice a pop-up showing all the fields and their values. While all this information is great, it can distract from your true purpose of showing rent as a percentage of income. Hover over **RentPercentOfIncomeSacramentoACS2016** again, and you'll see an icon that looks like three dots (an ellipsis); click it, and then click **Configure Pop-up**.

14. The pane that appears is where you can configure your pop-ups. Right now, it is set to display **A list of attributes**; you want to change the pop-up to only show the field **RentPercentage**. To do this, click **Configure Attributes,** and a new window will pop-up. Uncheck every field except for **RentPercentage,** and click **OK,** then **OK** again.

15. Now that you have your pop-ups configured, it's time to polish off the map for sharing. **RentPercentOfIncomeSacramentoACS2016** is a descriptive title for us, but to the non-GIS user, it may be confusing. You will want to change the layer name to **Rent as a Percentage of Income,** and to do this, hover over the layer and click the three dots again. Click **Rename** and enter the new name.

16. Now you are ready to save this map and share it. Click **Save** and give your web map a title, some tags, and a summary. Choose the folder you'd like to save it in and click **Save Map**. Now click **Share,** and check the box next to **Everyone** (public). You'll notice that a warning window pops up. It says that the layer we published may not be visible, so you must update the sharing of that layer so it is set to **Everyone** (public), too. Luckily, ArcGIS Online is smart enough to detect this and change it for you. To change the sharing properties of the layer, click **Update Sharing**. Another window will pop-up, telling you that a shortened URL will be generated for sharing, and to use that link when sharing, click **OK**. Now you can copy the shortened URL and send it to people so they can see your map.

Summary

You have been given a lot of information about ArcGIS Online, and it really only scratched the surface of this complex platform. After going through the sections and the exercise, you should have a good grasp of what ArcGIS Online is, how it is structured, how to create a web map, and how to publish a feature layer from ArcGIS Pro to ArcGIS Online. Again, it is recommended to go to the help documentation for ArcGIS Online, found at `https://doc.arcgis.com/en/arcgis-online/`, to learn more about the platform and its capabilities.

In the next chapter, you will build on what you learned in this chapter by utilizing Smart Mapping in ArcGIS Online.

10
Leveraging Esri Smart Mapping

In `Chapter 9`, *Getting Started with ArcGIS Online*, you learned about ArcGIS Online and the power that the platform has to store and display your data. You learned how to take data you have authored in ArcGIS Pro, upload it to ArcGIS Online, and display it in a web map that can be shared with anyone. Now, you will learn about the smart mapping abilities that ArcGIS Online has to help you save time and effort in creating visually appealing and meaningful web maps.

In this chapter, you will cover the following:

- Leveraging Esri's smart mapping in ArcGIS Online
- Creating beautiful and easy-to-understand maps in just a few clicks
- Using smart mapping to help perform menial tasks to save you time
- Using a new cross-platform expression language called Arcade
- Creating new dynamic data from your data for use in symbology, labeling, and pop-ups

In this chapter, you will be using web maps and layers that can be found in the GitHub link provided at the beginning of this book.

Smart mapping

What looks good in print does not always translate well to the web, as your viewer's screen size may drastically differ from another. Sometimes your web map will be seen on a large desktop monitor and sometimes it may be viewed on a smart phone screen, so cartographic styling will be tougher. Unlike a paper map you author in ArcGIS Pro, you don't have control over the size of the map output.

Even though you give up that control, you have a lot more options available to you because the data your viewer will have will be dynamic. The viewer can pan and zoom around, turn layers on and off, and can even reorder items. Smart mapping is a tool for setting the cartography in your web maps. It is an automated tool that will look at your data and recognize what type of data you have and the types of values your data has in it. It will also prepare cartographic symbology for your data based on what the tool has seen. Smart mapping is dynamic in that, as you change attributes to symbolize, it will change its suggested cartographic symbology.

Understanding your data and the story you want to tell

Smart mapping, while smart and powerful, can only help if you know what story you want to tell with your data. Are you trying to tell the story of changing populations, median income levels, volume of traffic along a highway, zoning, or simply showing the location of your data? Depending on the type of story you are telling with your data, the way you use smart mapping will be different. Throughout this whole book, you have learned strategies to make your data cleaner, what colors to use, and how to layer multiple data sets so that you can see all your data. Take all these principles that you have learned and apply them while using smart mapping.

Using smart mapping

In this section, you will learn how to let smart mapping make smaller and more tedious decisions for you, saving your time and effort in creating good looking maps. Smart mapping will only show you symbolization methods that work with your data, so it helps you choose the correct methods of symbolizing your data. You will learn about the common ways in which smart mapping will display data and how it can even change automatically based on other colors within the web map in this section.

 Not all layers in a web map can have their symbology changed. You can only change the symbology of specific types of layers in ArcGIS Online. Map image layers and tile layers cannot have their symbology changed.

Choosing the attribute data to display

When you add a feature layer into a web map in ArcGIS Online, typically, it will use the default symbology that is stored within the service that creates the feature layer. To change the symbology of a feature layer, navigate to the **Content** pane and click on the symbol with a yellow circle, red square, and blue triangle under the layer name. If you hover your mouse over the symbol, it should read **Change Style**.

The **Content** pane should have changed to the **Change Style** pane, showing two areas identified with blue circles with **1** and **2** in them. This process of symbolizing is very much like the process in ArcGIS Pro, but it is made simpler as web maps don't have the power that ArcGIS Pro does. Number **1** asks you to **Choose an attribute to show**. You can use just one attribute or choose to add more attributes (up to five in total in certain cases) to be used in the setup of your symbolization:

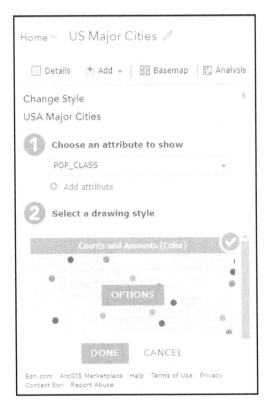

Figure 10.1: Style pane

You can also use a new feature in ArcGIS Online, Arcade, to create your symbology, but you will learn about that separately later in the *Arcade* section of this chapter.

Location

Sometimes you just want to see where your data is located on a map. In this case, you would choose the **Location (Single Symbol)** option in conjunction with setting your attribute to show it as **Show location only**. With this option, you can set a single symbol for all the data in your map. This would be useful to show locations like schools, roads, or census tracts. To change the options for location, hit the blue **Options** button under the **Location (Single Symbol)** heading. This will bring up the options you can set for your symbolization. To change the symbol, click on **Symbols** and depending on the type of geometry you are symbolizing, you are given options to change the shape, size, width, pattern, fill, outline, and/or transparency. You can also set a rotation for the symbol based on an attribute in your data by checking **Rotate symbols (degrees)**.

Point features have many different categories of symbols; it is suggested to go through them all to see all the options available to you. You can also use your own hosted image as a point symbol. It is recommended that you use a square image that is at most 120px x 120px.

Heat map

You can create heat maps when you select the location only or a numerical attribute of point feature layers by selecting heat map. Heat maps can be useful in certain uses, but when only showing the location, you can cause data quality issues, as you learned in Chapter 6, *All Maps Are Approximations of Reality*. You can also create a heat map with a numeric weight by choosing a single numeric attribute for your point data and selecting the **Heat Map** style. In the **Heat Map** options, you are given a color ramp suitable for a heat map. You can set how big clusters can be by using the **Area of Influence** slider.

A heat map is not a static calculation. When a viewer looks at your map and zooms in and out, the heat map will redraw based on data within the view extent. This can be unwanted behavior, so if you want to only show one level of heat map you must set the visible range so it can only be viewed at one zoom level.

Categories

When working with categorical data, you can use one or two attributes. When using just one attribute, you can use the **Types (Unique Symbols)** option. When you want to use two attributes, you can use the types and size option.

Types (Unique Symbols)

When you are only symbolizing one categorical attribute, you use the **Types (Unique Symbols)** option. This option allows you to create symbols for each unique value (it can be set to a maximum of 200). Typically, this option works best when you can group your data into 2-10 groups. In the options of **Types (Unique Symbols)**, a list is presented with the unique values of your attribute column. Smart mapping will automatically choose a color ramp and give you a count of the amount of features per unique value. If your data has more than 10 unique values, any value after the 10th will be grouped together with the **Other** value. If needed, you can ungroup a single value by clicking on the gray arrow to the right of the unique value. If you want to ungroup all of the unique values, click on the blue double arrow to the right of **Other**.

 You cannot undo these actions once they have been performed.

You can also change the drawing order of the unique values by clicking on and dragging the three dots to the left of the unique value's symbol. This can help when your categorical data is overlapping. To change the color ramp, click on the three colored squares just to the right of the **Count** column and click on **Fill.**

You can also change each unique value individually by clicking on the symbol to the left of the unique value in the list:

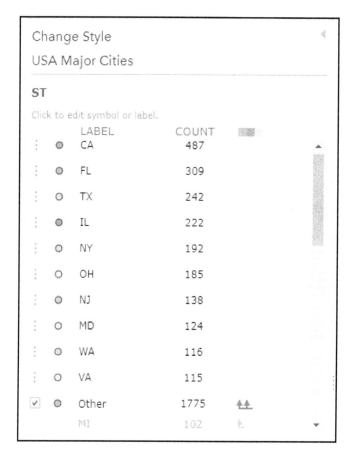

Figure 10.2: Categorical values in the Types (Unique Symbols) style

Types and size

If you want to show a numeric value in addition to the unique values set up, you would use the types and size option in your web map. For example, if you want to show the total population for each county in the United States and have each symbol colored by the state name to help differentiate larger proportional symbols that may grow beyond the state line, you would choose two attributes to show: state name and population. When you do this, smart mapping will give you only one option to symbolize your data: types and size. This option is essentially two styles grouped together—**Types (Unique Symbols)** and **Counts and Amounts (Size)**, which are just proportional symbols. You can change the options of each by clicking on **Options**.

Numbers

The **numbers** style has the most options available in smart mapping because you have the possibility to show up to five different attributes. These styles can be very complex to set up, but luckily, smart mapping makes it very easy for you to quickly choose the correct style for your needs.

Counts and Amounts (Color)

Counts and Amounts (Color) style is the basic color ramp symbology for when you want to show a single numeric value within your attribute. In the options for this style, you start by indicating whether you would like to divide the attribute by another in the drop-down menu to normalize your data. Normalizing your data is important as we learned in `Chapter 6`, *All Maps Are Approximations of Reality*. If your data is already normalized or does not need to be you can leave as **None**. The next drop-down menu asks you to select the theme of your data which are detailed as follows:

- **High to Low**: This theme shows a range of values from high to low. This emphasizes the highest and lowest values in your data, which works well for mapping things like the number of crimes committed in an area.

- **Above and Below**: This theme shows values above and below a specific value. This specific value would typically be average or zero if your data is both positive and negative. By default, smart mapping will use the mean of all your values in the attribute as the middle. This theme works well when you want to highlight locations where average income is higher or lower than the average of a larger geographical area.
- **Centered On**: This theme centers on and focuses on a specific value range. Any value that doesn't fit within the specified range will be made transparent to not draw attention away from the focused values. By default, smart mapping will choose the mean as the center and you can increase/decrease one standard deviation as the value range. This theme works well to remove outliers from your data.
- **Extremes**: This theme focuses on the extremes of your data; it essentially is the inverse of the **Centered On** theme. It focuses on data outside, which you can increase/decrease by one standard deviation of the mean:

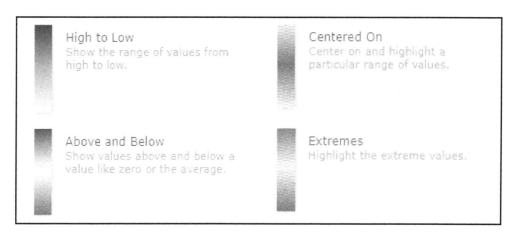

Figure 10.3: Themes for the Counts and Amounts (Color) style

Underneath the two drop-down menus is the color ramp with a histogram to the right side and the statistical mean symbol with a leader line showing the mean of the data. You can hover over the histogram to see how many records fall in each group, and you can also hover over the statistical mean symbol to see value. You will also see sliders on the left side of the color ramp and the value they are set at. Depending on the theme you chose earlier, you can have two or three sliders. You can move the sliders to change the value range for your theme. If you want a specific value for your slider, you can click on the number next to the slider and enter it in.

If your data has little variation and some large outliers, the histogram may have only one bar and your sliders may be so close that you can't grab them easily. You can zoom into your histogram by clicking the **Zoom in** button to the right of the histogram. To zoom back out, click **Zoom out:**

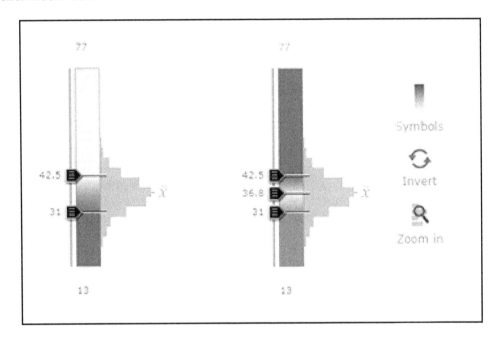

Figure 10.4: Example of color ramps and histograms

When you grab the middle slider in your color ramp, the other two sliders will move together with the third. This makes it easy to keep the range made by smart mapping or a custom range you created. If you want to change the default color ramp, just click on **Symbols** to the right of your current color ramp. It will bring up a selection of color ramps specific to your theme. To invert the colors, click on the two arrows in a circle. If smart mapping didn't organize the data the way you prefer, you can override the classification by checking the box next to **Classify Data** underneath the color ramp.

Counts and Amounts (Size)

Counts and Amounts (Size) style is basically the proportional symbol option that can be found in ArcGIS Pro. It will scale a single symbol based on the value of your attribute. When you view the options of this style, it will look similar to the **Counts and Amounts (Color)** options, but instead of choosing a color ramp, you are choosing the size of the symbol. You have the option of normalizing the data as well. You can use the two sliders on the size ramp to remove large and small values in case you have outliers. The sliders work the same as they do in the color option in the previous section. To change the symbol, click on the symbols to the right of the size ramp. Under the size ramp, you can set the min and max size of the symbol. Underneath that are the same tools you saw in the color style.

Color and Size

Color and Size style is used when you are using two attributes to symbolize your data. It is a combination of the two previous styles. The first attribute will use color and the second attribute will use size. This can be helpful when you want to clearly show two values using one piece of geometry.

Compare A to B

Compare A to B style is used when you want to compare two values together, for example, *A* as a percentage of *B*, *A* as a percent of *A + B*, or the ratio of *A* to *B*. This style is typically symbolized as a diverging color ramp.

Predominant Category

Predominant Category style is used when you have two to five related attributes that have the same unit of measure in your feature and you want to compare and show which attribute is predominant (highest value) and the degree of its predominance compared to the other attributes. Each attribute is given a color and the degree of predominance is symbolized by the amount of transparency that is applied. The **degree of predominance** is computed as a percentage of the total value of all attributes for that specific feature.

Predominant category and size

Predominant category and size style is much like the previous style but with the addition of the size as a symbolization option. The size is computed by adding the values of each attribute identified.

Time

When one of the attributes you are trying to symbolize is a date or time in a properly formatted field, you can make use of one of the smart mapping styles listed as follows:

- Continuous Timeline (Color)
- Continuous Timeline (Size)
- Age (Color)
- Age (Size)
- Color (age) and size, and color and size (age)

Continuous Timeline (Color)

Continuous Timeline (Color) style can be used when you are just trying to symbolize based on a single date/time attribute. This style will produce a color ramp and give you two theme options—**New to Old** and **Before and After**. **New to Old** will symbolize your data chronologically from old to new. You can also flip the color ramp by clicking on the **Invert** button so that you can symbolize **New to Old**. The other theme you can use is **Before and After**, which focuses on one date specifically and use a diverging color ramp to show dates above and below it.

Continuous Timeline (Size)

Continuous Timeline (Size) style can be used when you want your symbols to have their size based on your date/time attribute. This style is much like the **Counts and Amounts (Size)** style, but using chronological time.

Age (Color)

Age (Color) style is used to symbolize your features based on the amount of time that has passed since the date/time in your attribute by color. When you select this style, the date/time in your attribute will be used as the base date/time and the color symbol will show the amount of time, based on the units you choose, for a date selected by you. For example, this style can show the number of years that have passed since a house was sold. This can show patterns of where houses are being sold recently. If your data has another date/time field, you can also choose that to calculate the amount of time that has passed between the two fields. This style can only show one unit of time for its calculations, so you must choose from years, months, days, hours, minutes, and seconds. This style also has themes like the **Counts and Amounts (Color)** style mentioned previously in the chapter: **High to Low**, **Above and Below**, **Centered On**, and **Extremes**.

The **Age (Color)** style does not have a current date/time option, meaning that you have to select a specific day to calculate to. However, if you would like to calculate from the date/time someone views your web map, you can use Arcade, which will be covered later on in this chapter.

Age (Size)

Age (Size) style is very much like the **Counts and Amounts (Size)** style but uses a time attribute instead of a numeric attribute.

Color (age) and size, and color and size (age)

Color (age) and size, and color and size (age) style can be used when you have a two attributes, a date/time and numeric or categorical or even another date/time. These styles combine the **Color and Size** styles mentioned. An example of these styles is a web map showing service calls and the amount of time between a start and end date/time and the type of service call it is.

Smart mapping automatic colors

As mentioned in `Chapter 5`, *Picking Colors with Confidence*, color choice is important. When creating a web map, you may not have the ability to create your own basemap; so when using the Esri basemaps, smart mapping will detect the colors of the basemap and change your layer's colors automatically to make them noticeable and meaningful. The following is an example of how the colors change when the basemap is changed from topographic to dark gray:

Figure 10.5: Example of smart mapping changing colors based on basemap

As you can see, the color ramp flipped and made the blue a bit more saturated. This made the data pop-out on the dark gray basemap. Smart mapping was able to take a color ramp that may have not worked well with another basemap and change it automatically and seamlessly.

Arcade

One of the newest features for ArcGIS Online is Arcade. Arcade is a new, lightweight expression language that can be used within the ArcGIS environment to help with labeling, pop-ups, or symbology. If you have used JavaScript before, Arcade should look very familiar. This language allows you to create new data from your existing data on the fly and in memory. This means you can deliver truly dynamic symbology, labels, and pop-ups in your web maps instead of creating new fields and calculating static results.

When running through the smart mapping styles in the previous section, you might have noticed that when choosing an attribute, you saw **New Expression** as an option. This is where you would insert Arcade code to create new data from your data to symbolize. For example, Arcade can let you perform math functions on multiple fields to get a value that you use to symbolize each feature. A good real-world example of this would be if you had census tract data with the total population for 2016 and 2017 in individual fields. Using Arcade, you can take the 2017 field and subtract the 2016 field to show change in the total population. You can take it further by dividing that new value by the 2016 population to get the percent of change. Let's run through a couple of easy examples of using Arcade in symbolizing your data.

Using math expressions

Using the `Mapping With ArcGIS Pro Chapter 10 - Arcade Math` web map found in the GitHub repository (`https://github.com/PacktPublishing/Mapping-with-ArcGIS-Pro`) for this chapter, you will take the US counties data in the map and create a new dynamic value of percent of population change from 2010 to 2012 using Arcade. We will then make a choropleth map focusing on changes above 1% and below -1%. Consider the following steps:

1. Open the `Mapping with ArcGIS Pro Chapter 10 - Arcade Math` web map.
2. Click on **Change Style** for US counties.
3. Click on the drop-down under **Choose an attribute** and select **New Expression** at the bottom of the list.

4. The Arcade expression editor should pop-up:

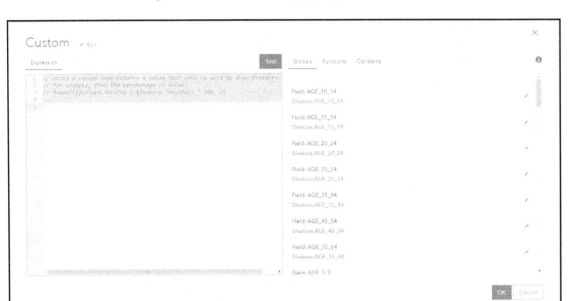

Figure 10.6: Arcade expression editor window

The Arcade expression editor is broken into two parts. On the left-hand side is your code block, where you enter your Arcade code, and on the right-hand side is a variable and expression list area. On the right-hand side, you will notice a list of the attributes in our feature layer and that it is under the **Globals** heading. This is the list of your global variables, typically your feature layer's attributes. Over the list of attributes, you will see two more headings: **Functions** and **Constants**. When you click on **Functions**, you will be presented with the functions you can perform using Arcade. When you click on **Constants**, you will be presented with a list of constants to use in your code, for example, infinity and pi. For this exercise, we won't be using any functions or constants, but it is recommended to see what is available for use once you become more comfortable using Arcade.

5. Under **Globals**, scroll down to the bottom of the list until you see **Field: POP2010** and **Field: POP2012**. Click on the blue text, **$feature.POP2012**, and you will see **$feature.POP2012** appear in the code block. You can click any blue text on the right to insert it into the code block on the left.

6. Since you want to find the percentage change between 2010 and 2012, you need to add a **-** and **$feature.POP2010**. Your code should now, read **$feature.POP2012-$feature.POP2010**.

7. To make this a percentage, you need to divide the value of your expression by **$feature.POP2010** and multiply by 100. To do this, put parentheses around the code you have and then put **/$feature.POP2010**, so now your code should look like **($feature.POP2012-$feature.POP2010)/$feature.POP2010**.

8. You now need to put another set of parentheses around your code and add `*100`, so that you can have a normal percentage number instead of a decimal ratio. Your code should now look like **(($feature.POP2012-$feature.POP2010)/$feature.POP2010)*100**.

9. Before you exit the Arcade expression editor, you need to change the name of this expression. Currently it's called **Custom**. To change this, look at the top-left corner of the Arcade expression editor window and next to **Custom** is a pencil icon called **Edit**. Click on **Edit** and enter `Population Change (Percent)` and click on **OK**. Click on **OK** again and the Arcade expression editor will close, and you'll see smart mapping automatically change to **Counts and Amounts (Size)**. Also, note that under **Choose an attribute to show** it says **Custom (Expression)**, which means that you are using an Arcade expression attribute. To go back and make changes to your Arcade expression, click on the pencil icon.

10. Proportional symbols aren't the best to show this kind of data, so click on **Select** under **Counts and Amounts (Color)** to change to a choropleth map. Since we want to show population change, we want to focus on values above and below **0**. To do this, click on **Options** under **Counts and Amounts (Color)**.

11. Change the drop-down menu next to **Theme** to **Above and Below**. Since the average of all your data is approximately 1.13, smart mapping has set the center at `1.13` and you want to change this to `0`. Click on **1.13** and enter `0` to set the middle slider. Once done, you will see that the other two sliders moved with the middle slider. However, these other sliders aren't set to what you want. Click on them and change their values to `1` and `-1`.

12. When you click on **Done**, you will now have created a map using an attribute born of other attributes in your feature layer.

Using date expressions

In the previous exercise, you found out about the power of Arcade to help create new numerical data dynamically from existing data. In this exercise, you will learn how to use Arcade to create a new date/time attribute to use in conjunction with a categorical attribute. You will be using the `Mapping With ArcGIS Pro Chapter 10 - Arcade Dates` web map found in the GitHub repository (`https://github.com/PacktPublishing/Mapping-with-ArcGIS-Pro`) for this exercise. This map has current active/open 311 calls to the City of Sacramento, CA. You will use this data to help create a web map showing the location of calls colored by what category they fall into and size them according to how long the call has been open for. Consider the following steps:

1. Click on **Change Style** of Open Sacramento 311 Calls to bring up the **Style** pane. Then select **Category Level 1** as your first attribute. Click on **Add attribute** to add another attribute. Select **New Expression** and when the Arcade expression editor opens, change the name from **Custom** to `Age of Calls (Days)`.

2. To calculate the number of days that have passed from the call until now, you can use a function called `DateDiff`. This function will calculate the amount of time that has passed between the two date/time values. To use this on your data, go to the right of the Arcade expression editor window and click on **Functions** and scroll down to find the `DateDiff` function. To find out more about the `DateDiff` function, click on the blue info icon on the right-hand side.

3. Click on `DateDiff` to add the function into your code block. You'll notice that it added placeholders inside the function to help you determine what to place where in the function. Since you want to calculate the amount of time from the creation date to now, now would be the end time. Since time is constantly moving, you want to be able to place the current date/time into this expression. To do this, you need to use the `Now` function.

4. Replace **endingDate** with `Now()` to set the ending date to the current date/time. Now you need to set **startingDate** to the **DateCreated** attribute. Click on **Globals** to bring up the list of attributes and scroll down until you find **$feature.DateCreated**. Replace **startingDate** with **$feature.DateCreated**.

5. The last portion of the `DateDiff` function you need to fill out is the time units to use. You will use days, and to do this, replace **ageUnits** with **days**. Be careful to make sure that you add the double quotes around "**days**". The reason for doing this is that the days value is a string in this function. In Arcade, string values must be in double quotes.

6. Click on **OK** and then on **Done** and you will notice that your data should have changed a bit. Now each point is colored based on the Category Level 1 attribute, and the size of the symbol relates to how long the call has been open. This type of map can help managers track what kinds of calls are open and how long they have been open for so that they can make better decisions.

Summary

In this chapter, you learned how to leverage the smart mapping tools made available in ArcGIS Online. You learned how color choice can be made easily and also making you aware of other colors within your web map. You learned how smart mapping suggests you to properly display the data you are trying to tell a story with. We also discussed the powerful new expression language, Arcade, which can help you create new dynamic data out of your existing data allowing you to create outstanding web maps that will get noticed.

Other Books You May Enjoy

If you enjoyed this book, you may be interested in these other books by Packt:

ArcPy and ArcGIS - Second Edition
Silas Toms, Dara O'Beirne

ISBN: 978-1-78728-251-3

- Understand how to integrate Python into ArcGIS and make GIS analysis faster and easier.
- Create Python script using ArcGIS ModelBuilder.
- Learn to use ArcGIS online feature services and the basics of the ArcGIS REST API
- Understand the unique Python environment that is new with ArcGIS Pro
- Learn about the new ArcGIS Python API and how to use Anaconda and Jupyter with it
- Learn to control ArcGIS Enterprise using ArcPy

ArcGIS Pro 2.x Cookbook
Tripp Corbin, GISP

ISBN: 978-1-78829-903-9

- Edit data using standard tools and topology
- Convert and link data together using joins and relates
- Create and share data using Projections and Coordinate Systems
- Access and collect data in the field using ArcGIS Collector
- Perform proximity analysis and map clusters with hotspot analysis
- Use the 3D Analyst Extension and perform advanced 3D analysis
- Share maps and data using ArcGIS Online via web and mobile apps

Leave a review - let other readers know what you think

Please share your thoughts on this book with others by leaving a review on the site that you bought it from. If you purchased the book from Amazon, please leave us an honest review on this book's Amazon page. This is vital so that other potential readers can see and use your unbiased opinion to make purchasing decisions, we can understand what our customers think about our products, and our authors can see your feedback on the title that they have worked with Packt to create. It will only take a few minutes of your time, but is valuable to other potential customers, our authors, and Packt. Thank you!

Index

CPSIA information can be obtained
at www.ICGtesting.com
Printed in the USA
BVHW080913270220
573450BV00007B/163

9 781788 298001